Dry Bo
Can Live

How to be part of a
Healthy Church

First published by O Books, 2010
O Books is an imprint of John Hunt Publishing Ltd., The Bothy, Deershot Lodge, Park Lane, Ropley,
Hants, SO24 0BE, UK
office1@o-books.net
www.o-books.net

Distribution in:	South Africa
	Stephan Phillips (pty) Ltd
UK and Europe	Email: orders@stephanphillips.com
Orca Book Services	Tel: 27 21 4489839 Telefax: 27 21 4479879
orders@orcabookservices.co.uk	
Tel: 01202 665432 Fax: 01202 666219	Text copyright John James 2008
Int. code (44)	
	Design: Stuart Davies
USA and Canada	
NBN	ISBN: 978 1 84694 282 2
custserv@nbnbooks.com	
Tel: 1 800 462 6420 Fax: 1 800 338 4550	All rights reserved. Except for brief quotations
	in critical articles or reviews, no part of this
	book may be reproduced in any manner without
Australia and New Zealand	prior written permission from the publishers.
Brumby Books	
sales@brumbybooks.com.au	
Tel: 61 3 9761 5535 Fax: 61 3 9761 7095	The rights of John James as author have been
	asserted in accordance with the Copyright,
Far East (offices in Singapore, Thailand,	Designs and Patents Act 1988.
Hong Kong, Taiwan)	
Pansing Distribution Pte Ltd	
kemal@pansing.com	A CIP catalogue record for this book is available
Tel: 65 6319 9939 Fax: 65 6462 5761	from the British Library.

Printed by Digital Book Print

O Books operates a distinctive and ethical publishing philosophy in
all areas of its business, from its global network of authors to
production and worldwide distribution.

Dry Bones Can Live

How to be part of a
Healthy Church

John James

BOOKS

Winchester, UK
Washington, USA

CONTENTS

To my wife Trish
who is the greatest encourager I know

Introduction

A pastor commencing a new ministry knew he faced a challenge with a regular congregation of only four. He set about visiting all the parishioners and was encouraged the next Sunday to see his congregation had grown by 50%! However, this most evangelistic of young pastors was not encouraged by everyone in the village telling him that they had given up on church attendance because the church was dead. Always imaginative, he wrote to the parishioners along these lines: 'The church is dead. Please attend the funeral'. At the appointed day and time, he was pleasantly surprised to see the church full for the service of thanksgiving he had invited everyone to. At the conclusion of a particularly lively service, when thanks were offered to the Lord for all that the church had meant in the past, the congregation was invited to form a queue to pass the open coffin and pay their last respects. Imagine their surprise when they each peered into the coffin to see their own reflection in a mirror suitably placed!

Certainly in many places at the present time, the church is a real turn-off to many people. They will say this without embarrassment. Many want Jesus Christ but want nothing to do with the church. Some others who call themselves committed Christians will not commit to a local church.

We have to be honest. There is a spiritual dearth in the church in many countries. I know what I am talking about, for I am a Welshman born and bred. I have exercised the whole of my pastoral ministry within the borders of Wales. Our memories are filled with stories of the Welsh revival of 1904–05. Today, most of the signs of that revival in the Principality are huge, empty and often derelict chapels.

At times the church has been very sick with what seemed to be a terminal illness, weakened not so much by attack from outside but by apostasy from within. On more than one occasion in history it looked as if God himself had abandoned it.

I believe that there are three major categories into one of which every unhealthy church will fit.

• Those churches in terminal decline. The best thing we can do for them is to help bury them with dignity. In the year of my presidency of the Baptist Union of Great Britain I received a letter from the members of a small church in the north west of England, asking me for permission to close their church. I did not actually have such authority but the letter came following a seminar that my wife and I had conducted in their church. (It had been the venue for a cluster meeting of Baptist churches.) They had been inspired by something we had said, and a hasty meeting of the few remaining members concluded that it would be better to close their church, so that they could join with a thriving fellowship nearby and release their very considerable resources to help further the Kingdom of God in other places. That took great vision and faith. If the local church is dead beyond resurrection, the best thing we can do is attend the funeral.

• Those churches that are very sick but following major surgery can recover. It is quite natural to get sick. Illness and health are not opposites. They are complements. We need not view disease as something that should not happen nor interpret it as a sign of weakness. Recognising there is illness is necessary in order to become healthy. A vaccination is an insertion of a weak, tired virus into the body; the virus causes us to suffer mini disease. If the body's balance were never tested by disease, it would never develop the immune system, the built-in defense against infection and disease in the body. I knew a church that had been in seemingly terminal decline for over 20 years. The situation was so serious that they invited a group to lead a stewardship campaign. For them, it was a way of carrying out a health check. As a result, they realized that they had to make some radical decisions. They had to face up to major issues including their theological ethos and lack of any missionary purpose. They are to be congratulated because they made the necessary changes and today are a strong and a healthy church.

• Those churches that are suffering what might be termed a 'dislocation' or minor disease. If they accept the diagnosis and prescribed remedy, they can get back on track.

So what is healthy? Individual differences are common. One person's medicine can be another's poison. It is difficult to define what is normal.

This book is written from my heart as well as my head and I want to affirm that I believe in the church. I have seen it at its best and at its worst as I have traveled the world. We live in exciting days for the church of Jesus Christ. It is growing on a worldwide scale more rapidly than ever before, but clearly all is not well in too many local congregations across the United Kingdom.

Have you ever sat down and honestly assessed your church's spiritual level? Do you find yourself becoming discontented with your church? Instead of writing it off, why not encourage the members to undergo at least a period of self-examination in a structured way? I am hoping that this book will serve that purpose: helping churches at least to undergo self-examination. The Divine Physician is ever present to help us in the task and he has given us rich resources.

He has given us the Bible as our textbook. In the Bible we discover principles of health and growth. Somewhere in every chapter of this book, as we look at the different characteristics of a healthy and therefore a growing church we always ask the question, 'What did Jesus say?' And then we find illustrations from the church of the New Testament.

It is true that we are also helped by a lot of research conducted by the former British Church Growth Association and more recently by the Institute for Natural Church Development. Christian A. Schwarz is President of the Institute, located in Germany. In recent years he has published several books on the theory and practice of church growth. In his book *Natural Church Development* he presents practical conclusions drawn from the most comprehensive study ever conducted on the causes of church growth – more than 1,000 churches, in 32 countries on all five continents, took part in this project. The conclusions reached are highly significant, particularly for the church in Europe. What is most interesting is that church growth occurs neither by accident nor according to a formula but is based on biblical principles. It is these principles that we will explore.

Another mighty resource that God has given is the presence and power of his Holy Spirit. The Holy Spirit, given to inspire the writing of scripture, is the same Spirit that will help us to understand, interpret and apply it to our situations. God has provided everything we need for a healthy church but we do not use the resources provided. Here in Wales we have a Welsh word *'hwyl'*. It can be used as a word to bid farewell to someone but is often associated with spontaneous and heartfelt fervor in worship. It actually means the 'setting of the sail'. What powerful imagery this is! God's Spirit blows, and all we have to do is set the sail and let him move us where he will. It is not our responsibility to make the wind blow but to recognize how God is working and to become partners with him. It sounds easy but it takes great skill to sail even the smallest of dinghies.

God's Spirit is moving all over the world and accomplishing great things. My prayer is that we might learn how to trim the sails and experience something of a mighty work of God throughout the world or that we might share the prophet Ezekiel's vision of a valley of dry bones that came alive and formed a vast army.

John James
Penarth 2009

Chapter 1

God's Strategy is Resurrection

'Dry Bones' or 'Dem Dry Bones' is a well-known traditional spiritual, often used to teach basic anatomy to children. The melody was written by James Weldon Johnson. Two versions of this traditional song are widely used, the second an abridgement of the first. The lyrics are based on Ezekiel 37:1–14, where the prophet visits the valley of dry bones and brings them to life by prophesying in God's name.

The chorus of the song is often used to teach children about skeletons:

Toe bone connected to the foot bone
Foot bone connected to the leg bone
Leg bone connected to the knee bone...

Ezekiel's vision depicts the desolation, destitution and dereliction of the nation of Israel and promises the restoration of the nation from its captivity. It also speaks of the dearth of life and vitality in the church of Jesus Christ.

The bones here speak of death. Paul tells us that until the Holy Spirit quickens men and women into spiritual life, they are 'dead in trespasses and sins' (Ephesians 2:1 King James Version). This can be true of your husband, your wife, your parents or your office colleagues. Though full of life physically, they can be dead spiritually. Similarly a church can seem to be alive due to much activity and even a reputation for high achievement. There was a church in Asia Minor called Sardis that had a reputation for being alive but the risen Christ said of it, 'You are dead. Wake up!' (Revelation 3:1–2).

Unbleached bones may have a purpose, but when 'very dry' (Ezekiel 37:2) they are worthless; it only remains for them to be gathered and burned. Similarly, the dead church is spiritually useless. Maybe this explains the sense of hopelessness in many failing congregations. 'Our bones are dried up and our hope is gone; we are cut off' (Ezekiel 37:11).

Jesus said, 'I will build my church, and the gates of Hades will not overcome it' (Matthew 16:18). Although many people in the twenty-first century have written the church off, it is still God's instrument for bringing his Kingdom in. All we have to do in response to God's ability is to discover his strategy for our church and follow it.

I commenced my full-time Christian ministry in 1968 as an enthusiastic pastor-evangelist. Yet within a year I was so overwhelmed by the many social problems on my urban patch that I sometimes felt that my wife and I were no more than an extension of the local social services. Nevertheless we learnt lessons about serving the community that have stood us in good stead for the rest of our ministry. Do not miss the word 'overwhelmed'. We were overwhelmed by the sheer size of the task and it became obvious that unless we had a strategy we would be distracted from our calling and purpose.

In parts of the United Kingdom a certain video is shown to police officers during their training. The film shows a bus crashing on the high street of a town. As a constable moves towards the scene of the crash he is interrupted by a high-speed car rushing through the same high street and stopping suddenly outside a bank. Armed men get out of the car and move towards the bank. The constable has a dilemma. As he takes a moment to think about his response, he hears over his radio that there is a bomb scare at the bus station at the end of the high street. The policeman, now facing a trilemma, is left frozen as the video ends. The question is then put to the trainee police officers: 'What would you do?' On one occasion a bright student replied, 'I would take off my uniform and merge with the crowd.' This sounds like good sense but it is not an appropriate strategy.

The Model Church
The early church in Jerusalem is the biblical model. The infant fellowship is described in Acts chapter 2:

They devoted themselves to the apostles' teaching and to the fellowship, to the breaking of bread and to prayer. Everyone was filled with awe, and many wonders and miraculous signs were done by the apostles. All the believers were together and had everything in common. Selling their possessions and goods, they gave to anyone as he had need. Every day they continued to meet together in the temple courts. They broke bread in their homes and ate together with glad and sincere hearts, praising God and enjoying the favour of all the people. And the Lord added to their number daily those who were being saved.
Acts 2:42–47

This has been called 'a lightning summary of the characteristics of the early church'.

- It was a learning church
- It was a fellowshipping church
- It was a praying church
- It was a worshiping church
- It was a sharing church
- It was a witnessing church
- It was an exciting church
- It was a happy church

What is more, it was all of these things at the same time. The early believers had discovered a harmony and strategy that enabled them to reach up, to reach out and to reach in.

Of course it wasn't a perfect church. The New Testament tells the story, warts and all. But when things went wrong they had the leadership, strategy and will to put them right.

The Muddled Church

Contrast that model church with the muddle we often find ourselves in. I cannot remember the number of times over the years that I have heard internationally respected church leaders say, 'The primary mission of the church is such-and-such...' What they are actually doing is sharing their own passion. What concerns me is that someone else's passion too often becomes another person's bandwagon. Below are some of the statements made:

- 'The primary task of the church is evangelism.' Who can deny that people without Christ are lost and facing a lost eternity? But some would argue...
- 'The primary task of the church is social action.' How can we preach the Good News until we are demonstrating it? Still others add their voices...
- 'The primary task of the church is worship.' The Westminster Confession does after all say, 'The chief end of man is to glorify God and to enjoy him forever'. Others will want to argue that...
- 'Fellowship should be the primary focus.' Yet others claim that...
- 'Signs and wonders are the missing dimension.'

Conferences have been held on these and many other aspects of church life, and many Christians come away feeling that if they could only get that part of church life right, everything else would be perfect.

But there is no single factor which makes a church healthy or will guarantee life and growth. A healthy church is a church that recognizes the importance of devoting itself to all of the qualities in the model New Testament church. We cannot afford to overlook any one area.

Christian Schwarz writes:

> The widespread claim that 'church growth is exclusively a matter of prayer' is simply not true. Such a statement makes absolute one element of the quality characteristics, 'passionate spirituality', at the expense of all the others. If this claim were true, it would mean that church development is possible without cultivating love, without making use of spiritual gifts and without evangelism. This viewpoint is not only empirically untenable; it is also contrary to scripture and thus a false teaching. Much prayer but little love, few gifts, and no evangelism? That would be strange indeed! Examples like this demonstrate once again the inherent contradictions of the 'super-spiritual paradigm'. Neither small groups, nor worship services, neither leadership nor structures, nor any other element is 'the' key to church growth. 'The' key is found in the harmonious interplay of all eight elements. We should be wary of advice to follow one person's pet emphasis to the exclusion of the other quality characteristics.[1]

Bringing It All Together
A vibrant, healthy church knows why it exists and what God has called it into being for.

Purpose
It is fashionable today, as in industry and education, for churches to have a mission statement. This is normally a memorable phrase that expresses the purpose for our being.

A library of books has already been written on this subject. The best of them to my mind are *The Purpose Driven Church* by Rick Warren, *Transitioning: Leading a Church Through Change* by Dan Southerland and *Releasing Your Church to Grow* by David Beer. I recommend all three books. In his last chapter David Beer tells the story of ten churches, all of which might be described as purpose driven churches.

Your church is unlikely to fulfill God's purpose for it unless you are open to change. Healthy churches are not only open to change but successfully manage the change they believe the Holy Spirit requires. They are also willing to release the resources to implement change.

David Beer writes:

> Spend time studying, reflecting and praying. Unless you are willing to give time to knowing God's purpose and how to fulfil it, intentional change probably won't happen. A new vision for the local church comes from the heart of the leader, which is why many churches today invite their clergy to take sabbaticals. Some denominations strongly advise their ministers to take a three-month sabbatical every seven years. If you are the team leader – pastor, vicar, minister, elder – this is a great opportunity to spend time reflecting, studying and praying about your own ministry and the life and ministry of your church.[2]

Once you are clear in your own mind, you need to appoint a small group of people to think through the purpose of the church. The aim of this activity is educational, to hammer out as a group what you feel the purpose of the church should be. This will involve Bible study, looking at the characteristics of the church and its work in the New Testament.

As the group puzzles over and prays about the application of these New Testament concepts to the life of their own church and to themselves today, there will be a growing awareness of what God calls his children to be as a gathered community, a church.

I was senior minister at Tabernacle Baptist Church, Penarth for 26 years and throughout that period we had set objectives and aims. For me it has been important to keep them constantly under review. When I retired, the purpose statement read, 'To reflect God's love in our church, community and world'. We added to that another statement expressing our calling: 'Our calling is to build up Christ's church, to reach the lost and to extend God's Kingdom first in the Penarth area, then wherever our committed disciples live and work.'

These statements were discussed and worked out by our Leadership Council and then accepted by the congregation. They were printed in large format in the foyer of our church and I hope they were indelibly inscribed on the minds and hearts of all the committed disciples.

It is not good enough to borrow someone else's purpose statement because the value of the exercise is in working it out as a group activity, so that people feel involved in the very words and concepts which they then have to commend to the wider church membership.

Aims

Having defined our purpose, it is then necessary to set down the particular areas of church life, and how these will work towards fulfilling our basic purpose. Throughout this book, I set out the strategic aim as we have worked it out in the local church. This book has been written with the members and leaders of the local church in mind. Let me stress how to bring these various elements together.

1. Sustain personal faith

Here we are talking about the making of disciples. There are a number of ways in which we seek to do this.

i. By discipling. If we are to reach every person in our village, town or parish and to make disciples of them, each existing disciple needs to be equipped for the task. The only way we can approach this mammoth task is not by adding people to our congregation, but by multiplying them. In other words, as part of people's nurture we need to bring them to a point of Christian maturity where they can also bring in their friends and family.

We developed a course suitable for our own people based on Rick Warren's *The Life Development Process*. It is an introduction to the concept of discipleship cycles, using the 'baseball diamond' as a model of Christian maturity. It looks at the process from conversion through discipleship and releasing into ministry as we see it in the ministry of Jesus, the early church and the contemporary setting. Disciples are invited to join the course, going from base to base.

- First base – Knowing Christ
- Second base – Growing in Christ
- Third base – Serving Christ
- Fourth base – Sharing Christ

ii. By worshiping. I have discovered that what happens on a Sunday really does determine how our people feel for the rest of the week. That is why every local church needs to agree the elements and the ethos of their worship to determine how best to equip the people of God to be disciples where they are.

iii. By teaching. I believe in expository preaching. Someone has said that there is only one thing that will ever take the place of great preaching and that is greater preaching. Preaching is primary, and expository preaching paramount. Without any question, the prime need of the twenty-first century is to return to the biblical injunction to 'preach the Word' (2 Timothy 4:2). I have been mentored in my preaching by the late Rev. Dr Stephen Olford. His definition of expository preaching is 'the presentation of biblical truth, derived from and transmitted through a historical, grammatical and Spirit-guided study of a passage in its context, which the Holy Spirit applies first to the life of the preacher and then through him to his congregation'.

It is preaching of this caliber and content that I am committed to. Preaching changes the direction of life – corporate and personal.

I am also committed to small groups. I believe that this is the best context for the application of the Word of God. For that reason I have been committed to producing quality material for small groups.

iv. By pastoral care. We share in later chapters how we attempt to provide this principally through small groups. However it is done, people need to feel loved and cared for. In times of joy and sorrow the family of the church needs to be there for its disciples.

v. By envisioning for mission. We need to keep the purpose and calling of the church before the people. There is the need to define our vision and our values in ways that every member can relate to. Many Christians are becoming aware of the need for the church to become more missionary-minded and less mainte-nance-orientated. Every member has a role to play in fulfilling the Great Commission through word and deed.

2. Support Christian family life

We all know that something is wrong with the home. Jesus talked about two men who were building their houses. One built his house on a solid rock foundation. When the storms and the winds came, his house stood firm. The other man built his house on sand. When the storms came, his house crumbled and fell. Too many homes today are built on sand; they do not have the right foundation. When the floods of sorrow, the waves of temptation, and the gales of adversity come, homes too often come crashing down. Christian homes should be different. Statistically it has been shown that there is no difference, that Christian homes are as likely to break up as non-Christian homes. This ought not to be. We need to encourage disciples to make this the order of their priorities: God first, family relation-ships second, and church third. The very mention of family will cause some hackles to be raised so let me spell out what I mean.

i. Model family life. We must not overburden parents. Yes, they have gifts and ministries to exercise but their first calling is to raise their children in the Christian way. There must be teaching on family life, on relationships and on being a single parent. Special provision needs to be made for supporting single parents. We need to provide support for all families by means of toddlers' groups, latchkey clubs and holiday clubs. Of course we have already recognized that not every church can provide for every need but churches working together in an area should be able to provide a distinctively Christian service. I thank God for those churches that are committed to reaching men with the Good News. We have seen more than a few husbands and fathers reached through creative means.

ii. Affirm the singles. According to the latest UK statistics, 36% of all adult men and 38% of all adult women are walking through life alone. With longer life expectancy and the escalating divorce rate, the number is constantly rising. For some singles, life is not easy. Many of them do not live alone by choice. Bereavement, unwanted divorce, or simply never having found the 'right' person, has left them to face the pressures of life on their own. Even those who choose singleness are sometimes frustrated. They miss the companionship, moral support and encouragement that marriage should offer. Furthermore, many singles have encountered difficulties in being accepted even by their own church family.

It is time for us to address the needs of those who are in most danger of walking alone – whether widowed, divorced or single by choice. The Bible is clear: God's purpose for his children, whatever their circumstances, is to know love, joy and peace and true fulfillment. I have discovered that single people are God's special gift to the local church. The Apostle Paul, for example, extolled the advantages of being single: 'I would like you to be free from concern. An unmarried man is concerned about the

Lord's affairs – how he can please the Lord' (1 Corinthians 7:32). Those believers given the gift of singleness and thus unencumbered by responsibility for a married partner and family have more freedom to fulfill their calling in the Lord. We need to recognize the special place they have in the Body of Christ and protect them from the insensitivity of would-be matchmakers.

iii. Do not neglect the elderly. Some may look forward to retirement from their place of work but there is no retirement in the Kingdom of God. There is just retraining for new tasks. The advent of early retirement has proved a blessing to many churches. Here is a resource for the Kingdom of God that must not be overlooked.

iv. Discover and release the gifts of children. Christian children are not the church of tomorrow but are part of the church today and need to be encouraged to find their place and use their gifts like every other Christian.

v. See the church as a family. Everyone has something to contribute to the work of the church. We realize we can only fulfill our purpose and achieve our aims if each of us plays a part in the work, prays for it, pays for it and speaks up for it. Being a family is the basis of our being. We need to guard against anyone being overburdened with responsibility. There is wisdom in proposing that jobs are done for an agreed period of time. We must use some principles of management to share both the tasks and the responsibilities for achieving our aims. We do not want to exhaust our energies in constant committee meetings, and so, as far as possible, individuals should be responsible for particular areas of work, helped by groups of people when necessary.

We recognize too that the local church is only part of the family of God. It is important for us to work closely with Christians of other denominations and traditions.

3. Support outgoing spirituality

Here we are talking about the life of prayer. In chapter ten, which focuses on prayer, I refer to finding creative means of praying together. Because it is one of our stated aims to encourage the development of small groups alongside the Sunday worship services, we ask would-be disciples to make the small group a priority meeting. This is an ideal setting for disciples to be creative in trying new ways of praying together.

Recognize, however, that it is important for the whole church to have times when they can meet specifically to pray together. Perhaps you could meet once a month for 'A Call to Prayer'. This should be a means of trying to keep praying together fresh, meaningful and open to the leading of the Holy Spirit.

Those who feel called to evangelism or community involvement should be encouraged regularly to take other members on 'prayer walks', during which prayer can be made at strategic places in the town. We have prayed outside the town hall, other churches, the Jehovah's Witnesses Kingdom Hall, and popular pubs and clubs. It is important to pray at the end of a road before you do door-to-door visiting. In these ways we encourage people to pray at all times as we go about our normal life. We have invited prayer requests from the community and provided a prayer box in the foyer of the church center for people to deposit their requests. They are then displayed on the prayer board. Why is it that so many churches hold a service of valediction for missionaries going overseas but seldom do so for other key workers in our own communities? Every year I organized a valedictory service for teachers and educationalists on 'Education Sunday'. You could observe 'Healthcare Sunday' by recognizing and praying for all those who are engaged in medical care in the community. Seize every opportunity to encourage incarnational mission. The presence of Christian disciples in the world is to be as salt and light. We need to find ways of reinforcing the truth that we are all missionaries.

It is when every member witnesses that we see the church growing significantly.

4. Set up community occasions

The church is a community within a community. Every local church must seek ways of serving that community. There is something special about creating occasions for social interaction.

It was with some trepidation that we arranged our first sports night. It felt like entering the lions' den when I went into the local rugby club to ask if we could hold a joint sports night. We challenged the club members to play us at their games: pool, darts, skittles and a quiz, and we offered to perform a cabaret at the end of the evening. The club steward was so keen to demonstrate their superiority that he offered to lay on a buffet supper. It was embarrassing, though very satisfying, to beat them at their games and then have the opportunity to present the Good News in a light-hearted way through the cabaret. The Kingdom of God that night was advanced.

We have enjoyed similar experiences with barn dances, line dances, Halloween alternatives and a host of other social gatherings. The social element is, I believe, one of the reasons for the success of the Alpha Course. The weekly supper is a winner. People relax and conversation ensues. Relationships are formed and bridges between the two communities are built. Parent–teacher associations, school governors' meetings, residents' associations, sailing clubs, golf clubs and sports centers are all natural meeting places. Christians need to be involved in these for the sake of Jesus Christ and his Kingdom.

5. Select your missionaries

The church is the Body of Christ. 'It was he who gave some to be apostles, some to be prophets, some to be evangelists, and some to be pastors and teachers, to prepare God's people for works of service, so that the body of Christ may be built up' (Ephesians

4:11–12). Here is a picture of leaders with different gifts equipping the members of the church so that other necessary ministries can be performed. Everyone, from the beginning of their life as a Christian, should be helped to discover, develop and use their gifts. This is the way to build growth into a believer's life.

Rick Warren says, 'It takes a variety of spiritual experiences with God to produce spiritual maturity.' He suggests five questions we need to ask about whatever method we choose to help people to grow:

i. Are people learning the content and meaning of the Bible?
ii. Are people seeing themselves, life and other people all clearly from God's perspective?
iii. Are people's values becoming aligned with God's values?
iv. Are people becoming more skilled in serving God?
v. Are people becoming more like Christ?[3]

Objectives
Strategies must be subject to development and change. A process of review needs to be built into all strategies. Once purpose and aims are clear, it is then worthwhile to decide what particular objective you are going to concentrate on for a limited time, for example, six or 12 months. The routine things will be maintained, but time will be secured, we hope, to concentrate on a particular aspect of work. Your objective may be quite precise: perhaps to establish four house groups or a new way of doing your youth work. On the other hand, it may be less definable, such as improving personal relationships between the people on your leadership team. Objectives can be set for church life or the leadership group, or individuals can set their own personal objectives.

Write them down, check them from time to time and you will not forget what it is you are aiming for. At the end of the set period, review what has been achieved. Some people set themselves targets that are too ambitious whilst others are not ambitious enough. What is true is that if you aim at nothing, that is what you will achieve.

A healthy church has a clear sense of direction, seeking to find out what God wants and then to do it. Once you find a strategy that works, stick with it as long as it lasts. Meanwhile our focus must be on the Lord Jesus Christ, who is the resurrection and the life, and we must always be open to Spirit-directed change.

Chapter 2

Growth: A Sign of Life and Health

It is quite fashionable for young Christians to wear bracelets. On one wrist they wear a band with the initials 'WWJS' and on the other 'WWJD'. These are to be a reminder that as part of our discipleship we are constantly to be asking the questions 'What Would Jesus Say?' and 'What Would Jesus Do?'

We are familiar with the Great Commission of the Lord Jesus, instructing us to go to:

- Every country (Acts 1:8)
- Every culture (Matthew 28:19; Luke 24:27)
- Every creature (Mark 16:15)

He, of course, modeled this in his own ministry. The apostolic gospel was 'first for the Jew, then for the Gentile' (Romans 1:16). But we find it prefigured in the Gospels. Jesus concentrated on Israel during his ministry but there are a number of pointers to the Gentile mission that would later develop. The story recorded in Matthew chapter 8 featuring the Gentile centurion teaches that the concern of Jesus was universal. The Lord Jesus explained the significance of this encounter in these words: 'I tell you the truth, I have not found anyone in Israel with such great faith. I say to you that many will come from the east and the west, and will take their places at the feast with Abraham, Isaac and Jacob in the kingdom of heaven' (Matthew 8:10–11).

Add to that the growth imagery in the teaching of Jesus:

- The parable of the sower teaches us that we are to expect a harvest in the world. (Matthew 13:1-23)

- The parable of the shepherd and the sheep teaches us that we are not only to protect the flock but we are to grow the flock. (Matthew 18:10-14)
- The parable of the dragnet teaches us that we are to expect a great in-gathering. (Matthew 13:47-50)

In his teaching on the vine and the branches we are encouraged to bear not only fruit and more fruit but much fruit, and that which will remain. (John 15:1-8)

The parable of the sower is an illustration not only that we are to expect growth but that the condition of the soil affects the return the farmer gets. However, at the end of the parable Jesus then reminds us of another factor in farming:

> This is what the kingdom of God is like; a man scatters seed on the ground. Night and day, whether he sleeps or gets up, the seed sprouts and grows, though he does not know how. All by itself the soil produces corn – first the stalk, then the ear, then the full grain in the ear.
> Mark 4:26–28

There is a hidden work being done in the soil. The clue is in the Greek term translated 'by itself', from which we get the word 'automatically'. There would be no harvest without this constant element in nature. There is a power for new life and growth at work without human assistance.

Jesus doesn't define it here but he is drawing attention to the divine provision which makes up for our inadequacies. If we sometimes wonder how we will ever achieve anything (if the sower is so important), we must remember that we are not the only ones at work.

This is a timely reminder that Jesus said, 'I will build my church'. Church growth is God's business. He is the Sovereign Lord. Our responsibility, or rather our response to his ability, is to ensure that we are in the center of his will and are obedient disciples.

There is a hidden energy at work below the surface, as the gospel message is preached and enacted. This is the sovereign purpose of God. God will do what he promised to do. He will grant growth. The Apostle Paul put it like this: 'I planted the seed, Apollos watered it, but God made it grow' (1 Corinthians 3:6).

Sometimes we can give the impression that church growth is dependent on our making sure that we do things right and well. However, that is only a small part of the truth. The whole truth is that without him, our Lord Jesus Christ, we can do nothing. What we have to discover are the biblical principles he wants us to adopt. Throughout the Bible, we consistently encounter the principles of church growth. We must discover what they are and, with the Holy Spirit's enabling, put them into practice. With that in mind we can go on to see what makes for a healthy church.

Jesus of course encourages us to be discerning and not to be uncritical. Not all growth is good growth. It was Jesus who said,

Not everyone who says to me, 'Lord, Lord,' will enter the kingdom of heaven, but only he who does the will of my father who is in heaven. Many will say to me on that day, 'Lord, Lord, did we not prophesy in your name, and in your name drive out demons and perform many miracles?' Then I will tell them plainly, 'I never knew you. Away from me, you evildoers!'
Matthew 7:21–23

Dr Peter Brierley is a man whom God has raised up for such a time as this. As Executive Director of the Christian Research Association he has gained a well-earned reputation as a person who has done more than most to provide Christian leaders with resources and training to enable their strategic planning for evangelism and growth. In his book *The Tide is Running Out* he presents dramatic and disturbing conclusions which are the stuff of headlines. The fall in the average number of Sunday church-goers is accelerating, and many of those lost are children. At first glance it seems that churchgoing in Britain is, if not dead, then certainly in terminal decline.

Some Churches Do Grow

The above conclusions, however, do not tell the whole story. There is a sizeable number of churches that are bucking the trend and growing significantly.

The Kingsway International Christian Centre in Hackney, East London, is already Britain's biggest church, attracting 12,000 worshipers every Sunday and claiming a total congregation of more than 300,000 in 18 congregations.

The pastor of Kingsway Centre, Rev. Matthew Ashimolowo, a convert from Islam, came to Britain from Africa in the 1980s and started a church with a congregation of 11 adults and six children. By September 1992, there were 300 members who rented a hall at Holloway Boys' School, North London. His present building, a converted warehouse next to the Hackney greyhound stadium, has a 4,000-seat auditorium and there are plans to build a church center to seat 10,000.

When his church organized a service to mark the millennium in the Docklands London Arena, it attracted 12,000 people, more than attended the opening of the Millennium Dome across the Thames in Greenwich.

I cannot claim to have known such phenomenal growth in my own ministry but, after more than 40 years in ministry, I have seen growth in churches in all kinds of social settings. In March 2004 I was invited by Peter Brierley to speak at an event organized by the Christian Research Association: the Larger Churches Forum. In preparation I analyzed the statistics of

Tabernacle Baptist Church, Penarth from 1982 to 2002. During that time, by the grace of God, we received 703 new members: 426 by believer's baptism, 159 by transfers from other churches and 118 by restoration. I am always reluctant to tell my story because I know I am a debtor to grace. I do not deserve such blessing, as more than a few have been quick to tell me. The truth is that God loves to bless.

I believe the church can grow again, in any country, and I believe this not because of my own experience but because God has clearly stated, in the Bible, that he wants to grow his church. We will explore how it may happen.

The first disciples took Jesus at his word, and the evidence of the Acts of the Apostles is there for all to see. Just look at the performance of the New Testament church as recorded for us in this one book of the Bible.

Acts 1:15	The church has 120 members
Acts 2:41	3,000 new converts are added
Acts 4:4	A membership of 5,000 men plus women and children
Acts 5:14–16	Believers are now described as 'multitudes' (KJV)
Acts 6:1, 7	The church is said to have 'multiplied' (KJV)
Acts 9:31	The church continues to grow throughout Judea, Galilee and Samaria
Acts 10	The first full-blooded Gentiles are converted
Acts 11:20–21	'A great number' of Greeks turn to the Lord
Acts 16:5	The church grows every day in Asia
Acts 16:11ff	Europe is reached for Christ
Acts 21:20	'Thousands' believe

Even at a casual glance, this is pretty convincing evidence that the Lord wanted his church to grow. In fact, throughout the 2,000 years of church history, whenever attention has been paid to the health of the Body of Christ, whenever the Great Commission to make disciples throughout the world has been obeyed, and whenever the Great Commandment to 'love one another' has been observed, the church has grown.

During the first 300 years of church history, the percentage of professing Christians in the world population grew from zero to 10%. The tragedy is that for the next 1,500 years the church became sick and there was no measurable growth. That is not to say that there were no healthy Christians alive during that period – there were. The missionary-minded monks did a remarkable work but the church was sick and did not grow. However, during the nineteenth century the church of Jesus Christ knew the greatest period of growth in its history. It moved from 10% of world population to 33%. This was the result of the sovereignty of God in sending revivals and in raising up a missionary church.

The tragedy is that once again, after the revival of 1904–05 which started in Wales and spread to the world, the church in the West has entered a period of sad decline. I believe the reasons are clear, and the heart of the problem is the failure to take the teachings of Jesus Christ seriously enough.

The good news is that since 1958 there has been a turning of the tide across the world and numerically the number of professing Christians is on the rise again. May God grant to his church throughout the world a vision of ourselves as God's advancing army with the gates of hell already crumbling as our marching feet shake the ground! It is the clear teaching of the Word of God that, whenever the Body of Christ is healthy, it grows. Whenever it is in decline, there is some sickness or malady afflicting it. The purpose of this book is to help local churches in their diagnosis of what is wrong and to begin to see the mind of the Wonderful Counselor in putting it right.

The influence of Rick Warren's book *The Purpose Driven Church* cannot be overstated. One simple fact alone shocked and challenged many pastors, including me. He said that our problem today is not growth but health! You do not have to tell children to grow; just ensure that they are healthy and under normal circumstances they will grow all by themselves.

This does not mean that every local church has to be a growing church. We must expect the death of some churches as well as the birth of new ones. Kenneth Scott Latourette in *A History of the Expansion of Christianity* concludes that the story of the church over 2,000 years is not one of a steady progression; it is a story of advance and recession, not irreversible progress.

As Christian Schwarz says in *Natural Church Development,*

Every form of organic growth sooner or later reaches its natural limits. A tree does not keep getting bigger; it brings forth new trees, which in turn produce more trees. This is the biotic principle of multiplication which characterises all of God's creation... The principle of multiplication applies to all areas of church life. Just as the fruit of an apple tree is not an apple, but another tree; the true fruit of a small group is not a new Christian, but another group; the true fruit of a church is not a new group, but a new church; the true fruit of a leader is not a follower, but a new leader; the true fruit of an evangelist is not a convert, but new evangelists. Whenever this principle is understood and applied, the results are dramatic...Where multiplication processes are functioning, straightforward talk about 'death' is also permitted. Why should groups or even whole churches be allowed to die after they have run their course? This thought should not be threatening at all if the given church or group has produced four 'children', sixteen 'grandchildren', and fifty-four 'great grandchildren'! In God's creation, the genetic information remains and reproduces itself, though individual organisms die.[4]

Growth Much More than Numbers
We are aware that not every church that is growing numerically

is a healthy church. That is why there is the necessity for a spiritual health check to see if a church is growing in quality as well as quantity. The standard set is the New Testament church, not because it was perfect but because it sets out the principles by which we can measure our progress. In Acts 2:41–47 we see the scope of growth in various directions:

- Growing up in maturity (verse 42)
- Growing together in generosity and service (verse 44)
- Growing out together in community (verse 47)
- Growing numerically through mission (verse 47)

The healthy church pays attention to growth in every dimension and the following chapters will help you assess just how healthy your church is.

Chapter 3

Dead Churches are Made of Dead Christians

The young pastor who invited his parishioners to attend the funeral of their church did a wise thing in putting a mirror in the coffin so that they could see their own reflections as they peered in. A church is only as dead as the individuals who comprise the membership.

If we are to know healthy churches, the members must be healthy Christians. A local church is renewed only when its people know personal renewal. When Jesus Christ was confronted with a sick person he was specific with regard to his diagnosis and cure. He once met a man who had been born blind, John the Apostle tells us, and when the disciples saw this man they assumed that someone was to blame for his condition. Jesus dealt with them appropriately and without any accusation or prior explanation. He spat on the ground, made some mud with the saliva and put it on the man's eyes. '"Go," he told him, "wash in the pool of Siloam"… So the man went and washed, and came home seeing' (John 9:1ff). It seems to me that we always want to apportion blame for the state of the church today. However, I believe Jesus is more concerned about making us well. We need to come to the Divine Physician for a spiritual health check, accept his diagnosis and submit ourselves to whatever corrective therapy he considers necessary.

My car recently went in for a service. It was the first under warranty. I was very pleased with the car and unaware of anything being wrong; I thought it was perfectly healthy. Then the garage phoned to say that it needed £700 worth of work (I almost needed to see a doctor!). Amongst other problems, the alloyed wheels had a hairline fracture. The engineer told me this could have had fatal consequences. Thank God for check-ups!

A friend went for a routine health check and was shocked to be sent for further tests. He was even more shocked when cancer was diagnosed. He didn't have a clue. He seemed perfectly well. He is now on the road to recovery. Thank God for health check-ups.

Every Christian needs to undergo regular spiritual health checks. Before we diagnose what is wrong with the church, we need to ask the Lord to reveal what is wrong with our Christian lives.

A Proper Birth

Tragically, some people are never healthy, having been born 'unwell'. Some live with medical conditions all of their lives. Similarly, some spiritual sicknesses are caused because people have not been properly 'born'. Jesus said, 'You must be born again' (John 3:6), yet more than a few 'believers' have no testimony of such an experience.

Martha (not her real name) was a member of our church, faithful at all the meetings since her baptism 40 years previously. She was the wife of a deacon. After one Sunday evening service she was in tears. I arranged to see her the following day.

'I have been a member of Baptist churches for 40 years,' she told me, 'and last night my eyes were opened. Coming to church has been like going into a grocery store with my shopping list for God. Last night, for the first time in my life, I realized that it wasn't enough to be a baptized member; I needed to receive the Lord Jesus Christ as my personal Savior. I did so at the end of your sermon and I brought my much-needed shopping home.'

It was a wonderful transformation that we saw in Martha in the years following. She had been neurotic for years, unable to get through a day without her valium. That Sunday evening ended all that.

Tragically, it is not just members who need to be born again. It is sometimes leaders. I have witnessed six deacons converted in one church! The biggest shock for me came when I was conducting a mission in mid-Wales. A minister wearing a clerical collar came forward to the front of the church after I had preached. I thought he was coming up to help with the response from the people. When I asked him why he had come forward, he said it was to receive Christ as his Savior. That day, he made a public confession of his faith. We need to ensure we are functioning as healthy members of the local church.

A good place to start is in the Acts of the Apostles chapter 2. Here we have the account of the Day of Pentecost when 3,000 new members were added to the fellowship in Jerusalem.

Peter delivered what might be described as the inaugural address to the new community of believers. Like all biblical preaching, it centered on the claim of Jesus Christ as Lord. Peter declared the truth of:

- The Lord's incarnation (verse 22)
- The Lord's crucifixion (verse 23)
- The Lord's resurrection (verses 24–32)
- The Lord's exaltation (verse 33)

He was so effective under the anointing of the Holy Spirit that the hearers interrupted Peter's sermon with the question, 'Brothers, what shall we do?'

In Acts 2:38 Peter spells out the steps a person must take to become a member of the Body of Christ: 'Repent and be baptized, every one of you, in the name of Jesus Christ for the forgiveness of your sins. And you will receive the gift of the Holy Spirit.'

Notice the four steps that must be taken.

1. Repentance
True, the people of Jerusalem were feeling guilty about what they

had done to Jesus Christ. But repentance is much more than being sorry. It is agreeing with God about everything. It is a turning from self, sin and the power of Satan towards God. It means having God's point of view.

Janine prayed for her husband for 17 years before he turned to Christ as his Savior. I knew him for over a year before he made that step. We had many conversations and I knew that he was not far from the Kingdom. However, he kept putting off that commitment to God's grace.

Then it happened: one day, at a barbecue on a beach, he surrendered his life to Christ. I asked him what had held him back for so long.

'Well,' he replied, 'I have my own business, and the only way I've been able to make a profit is by buying things that "fall off the back of a lorry". I realized that when I came to Christ all this would have to stop. God changed my mind and in a flash I saw the horror of what I was doing and I agreed with God about it.'

The sequel to the story is that about 18 months later he brought me his company accounts and showed me that his profits had doubled in the full trading year since he had come to Christ. It pays to accept the Divine Physician's diagnosis.

2. Baptism

This is a sticking point for many people. It is often emphasized that baptism is merely an outward sign of what God has already done in saving an individual. It is therefore considered by many to be an option. Not so. It is a divine imperative and an instrument of grace. The issue at stake is obedience to the Master, but even more importantly than this, in the act of obedience baptism becomes a means of grace.

The verse being considered here clearly links repentance, baptism and the forgiveness of sins. Paul, writing to Titus, describes baptism as the 'washing of rebirth' (Titus 3:5) and in his letter to the Romans as burial and resurrection with Christ

(Romans 6:3ff).

God is at work in baptism. We call it a 'sacrament'. This word originally meant a vow of allegiance taken by a Roman soldier to his Emperor, but in the church it is used of those actions which mediate the grace of God. It is an outward and visible sign of an inward and spiritual grace.

This is much more than symbolism, for it achieves what it symbolizes. Not that it is a means of grace on its own, for believers' baptism is always linked to repentance and faith.

3. Faith in the name of Jesus for forgiveness of sins
'Repent and be baptized, every one of you, in the name of Jesus Christ for the forgiveness of your sins.' Forgiveness comes through faith in the name of Christ. When we are ill we see a doctor and he writes out a prescription. We look at the prescription and may have no idea what it means. Nevertheless, we go to the pharmacist and exercise perfect faith in taking the medicine according to the instructions.

In the spiritual realm, that is just the kind of faith God is looking for: a faith that not only believes that his Son Jesus Christ is the Savior of the world but that takes him personally for salvation and believes in his name.

The emphasis on repenting and believing in the name of Jesus Christ for the forgiveness of sins is because 'the name' represents the person. The name of Christ stands for his miraculous birth, his perfect life, his atoning death on the cross, his resurrection. All this is in his name, and when someone trusts their life to Christ and owes allegiance to him, that life is truly transformed.

Do you know what it is to be forgiven – to know that all of your sins are washed away? To have reassurance of this mighty fact: that Christ died to take away sins by the sacrifice of himself? When God forgives, he forgets; he blots out our sin. But forgiveness means even more than that. The word is translated elsewhere in scripture as meaning 'loosed', 'liberated', 'set free'.

Don't limit the extent of God's forgiveness. 'So if the Son sets you free, you will be free indeed' (John 8:36). What a great gift forgiveness is! To be no longer bound by sin, no longer tied by the chain of sin. We are liberated. That is what it means to be forgiven. Do you know forgiveness like that?

Still there is more. There is the fourth and final step.

4. Receiving the gift of the Holy Spirit

The Holy Spirit is God's gift. When we are converted, the Spirit of God comes in and takes up residence in our hearts. Our bodies become the temple of the Holy Spirit. What a wonderful miracle that is!

Christians sometimes fail to make the distinction between the person and the power of the Holy Spirit. Every Christian possesses the person of the Holy Spirit but that is not enough. We need to be filled with the Spirit and learn to walk in the power of the Holy Spirit.

I remember sitting under the ministry of Dr Martyn Lloyd Jones. It seemed as though he leant over the pulpit and looked straight into my eyes when he said, 'It is not enough to be saved. You need to know the baptism in the Holy Spirit.' It was some years after that experience that I entered into the glorious fullness of the Holy Spirit. Too many Christians argue about the terms 'the baptism of the Holy Spirit' and 'the fullness of the Holy Spirit'. It is a sign of the sickness of the church when we argue over such terms. I once witnessed two ministers getting so hot under the collar arguing over the 'baptism of the Holy Spirit' that they almost came to blows.

There is an impressive array of names of Spirit-filled and anointed Bible teachers who differ in their understanding of this term, 'the baptism of the Spirit'. Some, such as Dr G. Campbell Morgan, equated it with conversion. Others, for example his successor at Westminster Chapel, Dr Martyn Lloyd Jones, argued for a separate, distinct experience. And the dividing line, incidentally, is not to be drawn between the so-called charismatics and non-charismatics. There are charismatics who identify the baptism of the Spirit with new birth, and non-charismatics who distinguish the two experiences.

What is clear is that the New Testament believers had an experience that empowered them to do the work which Jesus began and which they were commissioned to continue. Sadly, this experience is often missing in the lives of Christians today.

Let me spell out the necessary steps to ensuring we are filled with the Holy Spirit. God made humans to be inhabited; therefore we can never be a vacuum. Either we are controlled by the Holy Spirit or by another spirit! It was to religious people that Jesus said, 'You belong to your father, the devil' (John 8:44). The Bible speaks of 'the spirit who is now at work in those who are disobedient' (Ephesians 2:2). So we must know experientially the person of the Holy Spirit in control of our lives. Do you?

• We must know the in-coming of the Spirit: '...the Spirit of truth. The world cannot accept him... But you know him, for he lives with you and will be in you' (John 14:17). The word 'accept' indicates that there must come a point when the Holy Spirit enters a believer's personality. This happens at conversion. Peter made this clear on the Day of Pentecost when he said to those who were convicted of their sins and need of the Savior, 'Repent, and be baptized, every one of you, in the name of Jesus Christ for the forgiveness of your sins. And you will receive the gift of the Holy Spirit' (Acts 2:38). Where there is repentance towards God, and faith in the Lord Jesus, the Holy Spirit comes into a person's life to quicken and to regenerate. Has that happened to you? Do you know a time when you actually received the Holy Spirit?

• We must know the in-dwelling of the Spirit: 'I will ask the Father, and he will give you another Counselor to be with you forever' (John 14:16). Jesus emphasized that when the Holy Spirit came he would live or stay with his disciples forever. The evidence of a genuine Christian experience is the conscious sense of the in-dwelling of the Holy Spirit. This is why Paul says, 'If anyone does not have the Spirit of Christ, he does not belong to Christ' (Romans 8:9). When the Holy Spirit enters the life of a person, there is the conscious sense of his presence that no other experience can stimulate or simulate. It is unique to a Christian.

• We must know the in-filling of the Spirit: 'Be filled with the Spirit' (Ephesians 5:18). The Apostle Paul is actually making a contrast here between drunkenness and the Holy Spirit's fullness: 'Do not get drunk on wine, which leads to debauchery. Instead, be filled with the Spirit.' A person who is drunk is 'under the influence' of alcohol, and a Spirit-filled Christian is under the influence of the Holy Spirit. This must not be taken as an excuse for inappropriate behavior by Spirit-filled Christians, for one of the fruits of the Holy Spirit is self-control. It has often been pointed out that the tense is important, for the verse might be translated, 'be being filled with the Spirit'. We must keep on being filled with the Holy Spirit, because too easily we 'leak'! The measure that we are living in repentance and faith is the same measure to which we are filled with the Holy Spirit.

But what about the 'baptism of the Spirit'? Judging by the amount of interest shown in this expression, you might expect it to be found on every page of the New Testament! Actually it occurs just seven times. And four of these are parallel references from the Gospels (Matthew 3:11; Mark 1:8; Luke 3:16; John 1:33). In each is recorded John the Baptist's prophecy that the Messiah would minister a greater baptism than his own water baptism. In Acts 1:5 the risen Jesus reminds the disciples of John's prophecy and the fact that its fulfillment is imminent. Later in Acts, Peter explains to the Jewish Christians at Jerusalem the significance of the Holy Spirit falling upon the Gentiles at Cornelius's conversion. Again he refers to John's promise, its realization at Pentecost and its relevance to his ministry among Cornelius's family and friends (Acts 11:16). In the final reference Paul states clearly that the Holy Spirit baptizes all Christians into the Body of Christ (1 Corinthians 12:13).

In each of the seven references, the term refers to Christian initiation – believers entering into the blessings of conversion. However, that just suggests that what some people describe as a second blessing should be available at conversion.

Ideally and potentially, the in-coming and in-filling of the Holy Spirit should happen together at conversion. Sadly, for a number of reasons this does not always happen. I was one that was not properly born. I was a professing Christian and had been in the Christian ministry for months before I came into the fullness of the Holy Spirit. I knew the person of the Lord Jesus Christ and the Holy Spirit's anointing on my life, but I knew little of the Holy Spirit's power. What a tragedy!

So the four steps are plain: repent, be baptized, believe in the name of the Lord Jesus for forgiveness, and receive the gift of the Holy Spirit. It is only when we have taken all four steps that we can ever hope to be spiritually healthy and to function properly in the Body of Christ.

When preaching, I frequently ask the question, 'Are you firing on all four cylinders?' What do I mean? Well, if you see each of those four steps as a cylinder which must fire if we are to fulfill our potential, you will understand what I mean.

When I was a small lad, in the early 1950s, my father would often crowd the whole family into our very small Austin 7. I still have a photograph of that car and I can't imagine now how my mother and father and all of us seven children fitted into it! One day my father announced we were going to Saundersfoot for the day, a drive of about 100 miles. We reached the hamlet of Red Roses, about 20 miles short of our destination, and had to stop. My father recognized the banging coming from the engine and announced that the 'big end' had gone. We were all put safely on the grass verge while he removed the offending big end. Having saved the oil in a biscuit tin which he always carried in the boot (along with the Primus stove, O blessed memory!), he put the oil back into the sump and we returned home. What an experience – driving 80 miles on three cylinders! Not an experience to be recommended, but we did it. It is possible to drive a four-cylinder car with just three cylinders operating – possible but not desirable. When I told this story on one occasion, a person related how he had once driven his four-cylinder car with only two firing!

The tragedy is that there are some Christians who see the four steps of Acts 2:38 as optional. Now it may be possible to be a Christian and leave out one or even two of these steps, but you will never fulfill your potential. So this is where our diagnosis must begin. We must examine whether or not we have entered into the fullness of all that God purposed for us in our salvation.

There is so much more to being a healthy Christian, but a proper birth is a must. We will now consider the next step.

Chapter 4

Use It or Lose It!

Followers of rugby will recognize the shout of the referee, 'Use it or lose it!' He is talking about the oval ball, of course; if play is slowed down deliberately by a player holding on to the ball, the whistle blows and advantage is given to the opposition. Too often we give the devil the advantage because Christians are not allowed to use their gifts.

David came to see me shortly after moving into the area and said that he and his wife Betty were considering joining our church but wanted to share a problem that they had experienced in every church where they had been members. David had spent the best part of 40 years in different evangelical fellowships but had known constant frustration. Because he was an engineer, it was assumed that his function in the church should be practical, so he was often asked to look after maintenance and electronic matters which he could easily perform. He did so gladly but nevertheless was in a state of continual frustration.

Using a simple method of discovery (which will be shared later in this chapter), it soon became plain that David had so much more to offer. Given his good grasp of biblical truth, and his (and Betty's) pastoral heart, he was an obvious candidate to enroll in our leadership training course. That was the beginning of a long and fruitful ministry.

The couple not only led a small house group with distinction but David went on to join our staff and later still to exercise a dynamic leadership role in a trans-local capacity: he was responsible for opening up a major partnership between Baptist churches in the UK and Poland.

What a pity that it had taken so long to help David find his true place in the Body of Christ where he could function effectively in his God-given roles! Healthy churches invest time and effort into helping every member to discover, develop and then release their gifts.

On the Day of Pentecost something else happened to the first disciples. Instead of being merely in the presence of the physical Christ, they were baptized into Christ himself. Two complementary but distinct things occurred at Pentecost: the Holy Spirit had put Christ into the disciples, and the Holy Spirit had put the disciples into Christ. It is for this reason that the Apostle Paul speaks more frequently of our being 'in Christ' than of Christ being in us.

The Body of Christ

Paul tells the church in Corinth, 'You are the Body of Christ' (1 Corinthians 12:27). He is not saying simply that the church is like a body – that a body with its many independent parts is a good picture of a church; rather he is saying that the church is actually the Body of Christ, in the sense that it is the place that he lives in and the means by which he works.

Our bodies are the means by which we express ourselves, by which we speak and work. When people are apologizing for not being able to be present somewhere, they often add, 'But I'll be with you in spirit.' Now if that means they are going to pray for the occasion then hallelujah! But often it is just an empty way of excusing themselves from being there. To be visible or useful, it isn't enough to be present in spirit. We need to bring our bodies too!

For the Lord Jesus to do his work on earth, he requires a 'body' in which his Spirit will dwell and through which he may operate. The Father gave him that Body on the Day of Pentecost.

Charles Price writes:

Everything that the Lord Jesus does in the world he does

39

Dry Bones Can Live

through his Body, through the church. He doesn't send angels to the mission field, he sends people! Angels would be a lot cheaper and certainly more effective, but they are not Christ's Body and it is Christ who is at work in the world. It would be more effective if an angel knocked on your neighbour's door to bring them the gospel than if you or I knocked on your neighbour's door! The neighbours know you, they hear you shout at the children they saw you throw the cat through the window and you feel your testimony to them is undermined. If an angel knocked on the door and just flapped his wings a little to give authenticity they would probably sit up and take notice! But that is not God's strategy in the world.[5]

Every single Christian is to be a living cell in that Body, and for the Body to function effectively every cell must live in harmony with all the other cells. There is no better description of the church as the Body of Christ than that provided in Holy Scripture itself.

You can easily enough see how this kind of thing works by looking no further than your own body. Your body has many parts – limbs, organs, cells – but no matter how many parts you can name, you're still one body. It's exactly the same with Christ. By means of his one Spirit, we all said good-bye to our partial and piecemeal lives. We each used to independently call our own shots, but then we entered into a large and integrated life in which he has the final say in everything...

But I also want you to think about how this keeps your significance from getting blown up into self-importance. For no matter how significant you are, it is only because of what you are a part of. An enormous eye or a gigantic hand wouldn't be a body, but a monster. What we have is one body with many parts, each its proper size and in its own proper place. No part is important on its own. Can you imagine Eye telling Hand, 'Get lost; I don't need you'? Or, Head telling Foot, 'You're fired; your job has been phased out?' As a matter of fact, in practice it works the other way – the 'lower' the part, the more basic, and therefore necessary. You can live without an eye, for instance, but not without a stomach. When it's a part of your own body you are concerned with, it makes no difference whether the part is visible or clothed, higher or lower. You give it dignity and honor just as it is, without comparisons. It anything, you have more concern for the lower parts. If you had to choose, wouldn't you prefer good digestion to full-bodied hair?

The way God designed our bodies is a model for understanding our lives together as a church: every part dependent on every other part, the parts we mention and the parts we don't, the parts we see and the parts we don't. If one part hurts, every other part is involved in the hurt, and in the healing. If one part flourishes, every other part enters into the exuberance.

You are Christ's Body – that's who you are! You must never forget this.
1 Corinthians 12:12–27 *The Message*

Finding our Place
For the Body of Christ to be in perfect health, all its members must function as they have been designed. Every believer must therefore know the purpose for which God has placed them in the Body of Christ.

The Lord Jesus knew his unique purpose and moved with determination to its fulfillment. He could say to his Father, 'I have brought you glory on earth by completing the work you gave me to do' (John 17:4). The Apostle Paul was driven by the same purpose declaring, 'The love of Christ compels us' (2 Corinthians 5:14). He too could say, 'I have finished the race' (2 Timothy 4:6).

The Bible is equally clear that God has a purpose for you and me to fulfill. No one else can do it. When God makes an individual he breaks the mould. We are stamped with individuality. Our primary task on entering the Body of Christ must be to discover God's purpose for our lives and do it.

> One of the reasons for frustration amongst believers arises from the fact that they do not know precisely what it is that God has fitted them to do in his Body. Joy comes when we discover our place in the Body of Christ, fit into the perfect pattern that God has prepared for us and contribute to the functioning of Christ's church according to God's design. Every Christian has at least one basic gift. You may feel very inept and inadequate, but believe me God has gifted you to do at least one thing well in the community of believers we call the church. So congratulations – you are gifted![6]

In 1982 when I settled as pastor of Tabernacle, I was pleased that Selwyn Hughes published the booklet I have just quoted from: *Discovering Your Place in the Body of Christ*. It has been a very effective tool in releasing ministries. Every year without exception since that time, we have sent people out to serve the Lord at home and overseas.

To quote from it again:

> The New Testament introduces us to three distinct streams of gifts which are listed respectively in Romans 12:6–8, 1 Cor 12:8–10 and Eph 4:11–12. After studying these passages for a number of years now it is my belief that each member of the Trinity assumes responsibility for the administration and operation for a particular set of gifts. In Eph 4:11–12 the gifts there are described as coming under the direct control of our Lord Jesus Christ. In other words they are Christ's gifts to the church. In 1 Cor 12:8–10 the gifts are said to be under the

control and administration of the Holy Spirit. In Romans 12, although there is no specific reference to these gifts coming under the direct control and administration of the Father, I believe it is safe to assume, on the basis of what I have said, and considering the precise nature of these gifts, that they are distributed and administered by God the Father.[7]

Accompanying this booklet, Crusade for World Revival (CWR) still publishes a chart to help you discover your basic gift. For some, the list of gifts there is too limited but C. Peter Wagner has produced a larger book, *Your Spiritual Gifts Can Help Your Church Grow*, in which 27 spiritual gifts are defined and discussed in some detail. I was surprised when I first read it to discover that celibacy, voluntary poverty and martyrdom are all described in the scriptures as gifts of God.

My theme as President of the Baptist Union of Great Britain (1996–97) was 'Make It Count'. One of the emphases made as I traveled the UK was 'Make Your Talents Count'. To coincide with that year, the Baptist Union of Great Britain issued a very useful leaflet, 'Discovering the Gifts of Church Members'. This resource is still available and makes the process of discovering your gift very accessible. A helpful chart is provided as an appendix at the end of this chapter.

Every minister should make it a priority to discover the gifts of church members and if the Minister doesn't, every disciple should pester him or her until he or she does.

Be warned, however, that you should not undertake this exercise unless the gifts discovered are used. Otherwise it leads only to an even greater frustration. There is yet another danger: we can so concentrate on the gift that we forget the Giver. Romans chapter 12, in describing those basic gifts of God, also presents another challenge. The Apostle Paul, after listing those gifts, adds, 'Don't burn out; keep yourselves fueled and aflame' (Romans 12:11 *The Message*).

43

Here is a call for a dynamic spirituality. When anyone receives the Lord Jesus Christ and becomes a Christian, a fire is lit within his or her heart by the Holy Spirit. By nature we do not have this fire, for there is no 'divine spark' in the heart of the 'natural man', but at conversion there begins to glow within us the fire of a new life. When we become Christians we obtain the fire of God's life, love and light, but having obtained the fire, the main thing is to maintain it. If a fire is neglected it will soon die down as it did in the case of young Timothy, so that Paul wrote to him on the need to 'stir up the gift of God' (2 Timothy 1:6 KJV). We may lose the 'flame', the 'glow' of our spiritual experience and we can through neglect or disobedience degenerate into a dull 'smoking flax' Christian. This is something to avoid at all costs. There are many Christians whose spiritual life is at low ebb and whose testimony is therefore ineffective. What a tragedy! Such unhealthy Christians make for an unhealthy church. Then the church appears as a corpse.

We need to ensure today that we are on fire for God and then make Charles Wesley's old hymn our prayer:

Jesus, confirm my heart's desire,
To work, and speak and think for thee;
Still let me guard the holy fire,
And still stir up thy gift in me.

Discovering Your Gifts
Read the following points, and mark yourself out of five for each. If you give yourself five, it will be one of your very strong points. If you give yourself nought or one, it will be one of your very weak points. Fill in what you give yourself in the same numbered squares.

1. I am good at listening.
2. I enjoy explaining things to others from the Bible.
3. I love preaching or talking about Jesus to a congregation/ group.
4. I am often used to bring others to Christ.
5. I enjoy administrative work.
6. I feel a deep caring love for those ill and a call to help them.
7. I am handy at most things and adaptable.
8. I am deeply concerned about the world and social affairs.
9. I am usually looked to for a lead.
10. I make helpful relationships with others easily.
11. Others are helped when I teach them things.
12. I love the study and work involved in preparing a message.
13. God has given me a love for others and a longing to win them for him.
14. I can organise well, clearly and efficiently.
15. Others find my presence soothing and healing.
16. I like helping other people.
17. I am active in service in the community.
18. In a group I am often elected chairman or leader.
19. I can encourage others and help bear burdens.
20. I love study and finding out facts.
21. My sermons have been clearly blessed to others.
22. I find my life is full of opportunities to witness to Christ.
23. I love doing office work and do it thoroughly.
24. I have sometimes laid hands on the sick and they have been helped.

25. I am a practical type.
26. I am very aware of the needs of society and feel called to help.
27. When leading something I put a lot of preparation into it.
28. I really care about other people.
29. I have patience in helping others understand Christian things.
30. I feel a clear call to preach.
31. I love to talk to others about Jesus.
32. I am painstaking about details in organisation.
33. I spend time praying for and with sick people.
34. I spend much time helping others in practical ways.
35. I feel God is at work in the world today and I must work alongside him.
36. I am good at delegating work to others in a team setting.

Add up the totals along each line and place them in the end column.

1	10	19	28	A
2	11	20	29	B
3	12	21	30	C
4	13	22	31	D
5	14	23	32	E
6	15	24	33	F
7	16	25	34	G
8	17	26	35	H
9	18	27	36	I

If your highest total is in column…

A – your gift is Pastoral.
B – your gift is Teaching.
C – your gift is Preaching.

D –   your gift is Evangelism.

E –   your gift is Administration.

F –   your gift is Healing.

G – your gift is Practical Helping.

H – your gift is Service to Society.

I – your gift is Leadership.

It is easy to mislead yourself and it may therefore be helpful to give a copy of this form to four of your closest friends and ask them to fill it in for you (i.e. changing the statement to 'she/he' and 'she is/he is' etc.) as honestly as possible. Don't show them your totals until after you have theirs.

This form can be rewritten to include other fields of gifts.

In every church there are rich resources, unrecognised and unused. It takes time, care, love and prayer for them to be discovered, to unfold and be developed, but given the expectation and help in a loving, creative fellowship, the most wonderful things emerge even from the most unlikely people.

The church is to be alive in every member as the body in which Jesus lives and through which he reaches out and does his work.[8]

Chapter 5

Your Epitaph

Andrew Carnegie's tombstone reads, 'Here lies a man who knew how to enlist the service of better men than himself.' John Maxwell in *The Power of Leadership* comments,

> I am drawn to Carnegie's humility, as well as his talent. He didn't try to do it all or own it all. He once said, 'I owe whatever success I have achieved, by the large, to my ability to surround myself with people who are smarter than I am.' He knew his own limitations, but that only spurred him on to find associates who didn't have the same ones.[9]

A healthy church will be led by leaders committed to empowering every Christian to minister within their gifting. Andrew Carnegie also said, 'No man will make a great leader who wants to do it all himself or get all the credit for doing it.'

There is no doubt that Jesus was the greatest leader who ever lived on earth. He lived for just 33 years and in three years he called, equipped and empowered his disciples to take the Good News across the world. No one throughout the history of humankind has known so many willing followers.

What are the secrets that we can learn from the Master?

Anointing
The Lord Jesus Christ was anointed for his unique calling. Commencing his ministry in Nazareth, he went to the synagogue and read from the book of the prophet Isaiah:

The Spirit of the Lord is on me,

because he has anointed me
to preach good news to the poor.
Luke 4:18

When the scripture reading was complete he added, 'Today this scripture is fulfilled in your hearing' (Luke 4:21).

It is not enough for ministers to be appointed to a position by the local church with or without their denominational blessing. The priority is to know that anointing of the Spirit. It happened for the Lord Jesus at his baptism: 'As he was praying, heaven was opened and the Holy Spirit descended on him in bodily form like a dove... "You are my Son whom I love; with you I am well pleased"' (Luke 3:21–22). He had a definite experience of being anointed for the task to which he was appointed. So must we.

In an earlier chapter we explored various terms relating to the person, the presence and the power of the Holy Spirit. Let me state it clearly, the fullness of the Holy Spirit is an essential and indispensable experience for spiritual leadership. Each of us can be as full of the Holy Spirit as we desire to be.

In-Filling with the Holy Spirit
The Lord Jesus Christ was filled with the Holy Spirit from his mother's womb. There was never a time when he wasn't Spirit-filled without measure, but it wasn't until he stood on the banks of the Jordan to launch his messianic ministry that the anointing came upon him in fulfillment of the prophecy of Isaiah.

I believe the anointing of the Holy Spirit comes at conversion just as the filling should and like the filling of the Spirit we need the anointing again and again. When the Lord calls us to perform a particular task or ministry we need a special anointing for it.

There are three interesting prepositions which Jesus used in connection with his teaching on the work of the Holy Spirit. A proper understanding of these helps in distinguishing the various aspects of his work.

- 'With'. We see this in John 14:17: '...the Spirit of truth. The world cannot accept him... But you know him, for he lives *with* you and will be in you' (my emphasis). The Holy Spirit is with everyone. It is he who before conversion convicts us of sin and introduces us to the truth of who Jesus Christ is.

- 'In'. '...the Spirit of truth. The world cannot accept him... But you know him, for he lives with you and will be *in* you' (John 14:17, my emphasis). At conversion the Holy Spirit enters our lives to enlighten our minds and regenerate our spirits. It is the Spirit in us that produces the fruit of the Spirit so we are gradually transformed into the likeness of Jesus Christ.

- 'On'. 'But you will receive power when the Holy Spirit comes *on* you and you will be my witnesses' (Acts 1:8, my emphasis). The Holy Spirit comes on us to clothe us with power, equipping us for all that we are called to be and do.

How can you ensure you are ministering on a full anointing of the Holy Spirit? The example given by the Lord Jesus gives us a clue and it is supported by the rest of the New Testament.

There must be obedience to the Word of God and dependence on the Spirit of God. Jesus went down into the Jordan to be baptized even though John resisted him. Jesus' response was, in effect, 'I must obey my Father'. There is an objective truth in the scriptures that we as believers in Christ must respond to with obedience. Such obedience should involve personal devotion, discipline and determination. Obedience is a must.

At the same time, we are not called to understand the Word of God through human insight alone, nor are we called to obey God's Word through human effort and strength alone. The Christian life is to be a life of obedience to God's Word, but also a life of dependence upon God's Spirit. God's Spirit provides illumination for understanding and enabling for obedience. We must hold in balance the call for personal obedience and the need for total dependence on the Spirit of God to do in and through us what we should not and cannot do ourselves.

My mentor Stephen Olford wrote, 'All Word and no Spirit and you will dry up, all Spirit and no Word and you blow up, all Word and all Spirit and you grow up.' So, however we understand the terms 'the baptism of', 'the fullness of', and 'the anointing with' the Holy Spirit, let us ensure that we enjoy all the provision that God made for us.

The question is: Have you the anointing to fulfill your appointment? I am convinced that seeking to fulfill an appointment without the anointing is an exercise in total futility.

Power

The Lord Jesus Christ empowered his disciples. So Christian leaders must empower the disciples of the local church. There are many ways we can do so: by believing in them, trusting them, encouraging them. But Jesus had a vision for them and inspired them to go after it.

Simon Peter's epitaph might well have been, 'The Sand man who became a Rock man'. When Jesus renamed Simon 'Peter', he realized the work that needed doing in him: 'Jesus looked at him and said, "You are Simon son of John. You will be called Cephas (which, when translated, is Peter [Rock])"'(John 1:42, my emphasis). Notice that emphasis: 'You are... You will be.' The Lord Jesus was inspiring and empowering Peter to believe he could be what he was being called to be. People saw in Peter instability, fickleness and fear, but Jesus saw what could be done through love and the divine power. People see us as we are, but God sees us as we can be in him. God's ability to give is limited by our capacity to receive.

Simon Peter was in many ways one of the greatest failures of the New Testament. He was, after all, the disciple that denied the Lord Jesus. This is not to say that Simon Peter was all bad. He was a strong man but flawed. He was a strong man intellectually, emotionally and volitionally. Peter had all the elements of a great personality yet these were not fused into consistency and strength. It was only the Lord Jesus seeing his potential that could help him to fulfill that potential.

Dr G. Campbell Morgan, referred to earlier, wrote, 'Simon Peter was a great man but lacked preciousness.' Then he pointed out how and why the word 'precious' was one of Simon Peter's key words in both his epistles. 'What is preciousness?' asked the doctor. 'We speak of jewels as precious stones, and it's an apt word. Every jewel is a combination of elements, welded into strength. This is what Simon lacked.'

Dr G. Campbell Morgan explained how geologists believe that rock is the result of processes. When various elements are mastered by that process, the result is rock. Jesus looked at Simon Peter and said, 'You will be called Peter, a Rock'. The Savior could detect all the necessary elements, but they lacked preciousness, consistency and strength. Jesus looks into our lives and sees what he can make of us, if we would submit to his integrating authority and mastery.

When did you last sit down with someone and become aware of the Holy Spirit's power in you, being communicated to them? Like the Lord Jesus and the Apostle Paul, we need not only the vision to share with people but also that inner energy to help them achieve it.

I thank God for a lovely man, now in the Glory, called Rosser Jeremiah. I have been preaching since I was 17 and at the age of 22 went to visit a newly planted Baptist church. Rosser Jeremiah, having known me for a number of years, put his hand on my shoulder, looked into my eyes and said, 'I believe that you are not only able, but you are going to be the pastor of this church.' And do you know, as he said it I felt power flowing from him to me. He had energy in him. He was empowering me, by sharing God's vision.

Servanthood

The Lord Jesus Christ modeled servanthood. Responding to a

dispute among his disciples as to which of them was to be regarded as the greatest, he said,

> The kings of the Gentiles lord it over them; and those who exercise authority over them are given the title Benefactor. But you are not to be like that. Instead, the greatest among you shall be like the youngest, and the one who rules like the one who serves. For who is greater, the one who is at the table or the one who serves? Is it not the one who is at the table? But I am among you as one who serves.
> Luke 22:25–27

The disciples were concerned for their personal dignity as authority figures but Jesus showed them the better way. It was he who washed their feet, modeling servanthood.

Those disciples did learn the lesson, for as we come into the Acts of the Apostles, we find them making it a priority to work every day serving the widows and orphans food. They did not regard such a task as demeaning to the apostolic office. They saw the need and they gave themselves to meeting it. True, they soon had to appoint others to take over this function but they did not ask anyone to perform tasks they were not themselves prepared to do.

The Apostle Paul set the same example to those he wanted to mentor. Writing to the Philippians, he spells out the seven-fold descent into greatness. It is the classic counter-cultural passage.

> Don't push your way to the front; don't sweet-talk your way to the top. Put yourself aside, and help other's get ahead. Don't be obsessed with getting your own advantage. Forget yourselves long enough to lend a helping hand. Think of yourselves the way Christ Jesus thought of himself. He had equal status with God but didn't think so much of himself that he had to cling to the advantages of that status no matter

what. Not at all. When the time came, he set aside the privileges of deity and took on the status of a slave, became human! Having become human, he stayed human. It was an incredibly humbling process. He didn't claim special privileges. Instead, he lived a selfless, obedient life and then died a selfless, obedient death – and the worst kind of death at that; a crucifixion. Because of that obedience, God lifted him high and honoured him far beyond anyone or anything, ever, so that all created beings in heaven and on earth – even those long ago dead and buried – will bow in worship before this Jesus Christ, and call out in praise that he is the Master of all, to the glory and honor of God the Father.

Philippians 2:3–11 *The Message*

Even secular lecturers today use this picture of servanthood as a model of management. This I am sure is in no small part due to the influence of people like John C. Maxwell who is a Christian. He is widely acclaimed in the world of business and commerce. Writing in *The 21 Indispensable Qualities of a Leader*, John Maxwell says,

When you think of servanthood, do you envisage it as an activity performed by relatively low skilled people at the bottom of the positional totem pole? If you do, you have a wrong impression. Servanthood is not about positional skill. It is about attitude. You have undoubtedly met people in service positions who have poor attitudes towards servanthood; the rude worker at the Government agency, the waiter who can't be bothered with taking your order, the store clerk who talks on the phone with a friend instead of helping you. Just as you can sense when a worker doesn't want to help people, you can just as easily detect whether a leader has a servant's heart. And the truth is that the best leaders desire to serve others, not themselves.

Maxwell then answers the question, 'What does it mean to embody the quality of servanthood?' and says that a true servant leader

1. Puts others ahead of his own agenda.
2. Possesses the confidence to serve.
3. Initiates service to others.
4. Is not position conscious.
5. Serves out of love.

Then he challenges us to reflect on it:

Where is your heart when it comes to serving others? Do you desire to become a leader for the perks and benefits? Are you motivated by a desire to help others? If you really want to become the kind of leader that people want to follow you will have to settle the issue of servanthood. If your attitude is to be served rather than serve, you may be headed for trouble. If this is an issue in your life, then heed this advice:
Stop lording over people, and start listening to them.
Stop role-playing for advancement, and start risking for others benefits.
Stop seeking your own way, and start serving others.
It is true that those who would be great must be like the least and servant of all.[10]

Thank God the teachings of Jesus are finding their way into the world of business and commerce! When will the leaders of the church of Jesus Christ learn and apply these lessons?

Vision for God's Purpose
The Lord Jesus Christ had a vision of God's ultimate purpose and went for it.
Vision is everything for a leader. It is utterly indispensable.

55

Why? Because the vision leads the leader. It paints the target, sparks and fuels the fire within and draws him forward. It is also the firelighter for others who follow that leader.

From the moment Jesus called his disciples to follow him, they knew the purpose for which they had been called. For instance, Jesus said, 'Follow me, and I will make you fishers of men' (Matthew 4:19 KJV). The Lord Jesus lived a purpose-driven life. From the first glimpse of our Lord at the age of 12 to the time of the cross, we see that his life was spent in unbroken communion with his heavenly Father. He shared those purposes with his disciples and, although they were slow to learn, they ultimately got the message.

In the words of John Sculley, former Chief Executive of Pepsi and Apple Computers, 'The future belongs to those who see possibilities before they become obvious.'

Of course, 'vision' for the Christian is different from 'vision' for the non-Christian. When the Bible says, 'Where there is no vision the people perish' (Proverbs 29:18), you might think that we have to dream something up quickly. However, the word 'vision' here is better translated 'revelation' as in the NIV: 'Where there is no revelation, the people cast off restraint; but blessed is he who keeps the law.'

The revelation has already been given in the person of our Lord Jesus Christ. 'But the Counselor, the Holy Spirit, whom the Father will send in my name, will teach you all things and will remind you of everything I have said to you' (John 14:26). This verse teaches that when the Holy Spirit takes control of a Christian's life a three-fold power is experienced:

• The power of revelation: 'He will teach you all things.' Here is the greatest distinction between human tuition and divine intuition. A person can be educated in the disciplines of the academic world yet be totally ignorant of God and his purposes for life. Only when the Holy Spirit comes into a person's life can he or she really know the things of God. By the term 'revelation' we mean 'all truth' which means truth without error. Some people claim to have 'extra-biblical' revelations, but such claims must always be tested by the body of truth, namely. the scriptures. Of course there can be fresh insights which the Holy Spirit gives us, but they must never run contrary to what is revealed in the Holy Scriptures.

•The power of recollection: 'He will remind you of everything I have said to you.' No psychologist or psychiatrist has yet explored fully the potentials and possibilities of the unconscious mind. But the Christian has the power of recollection through the operation of the Holy Spirit. This is a supernatural power and makes available a whole world of knowledge which would otherwise be lost.

•The power of realization: 'The Spirit of truth...will guide you into all truth... He will bring glory to me by taking from what is mine and making it known to you' (John 16:13–14). Everything God has ever promised his children in the Bible can be realized, in terms of personal practical experience, through the power of the Holy Spirit. For it is the supreme function of the Holy Spirit to make Jesus real to us, in us and through us in all the wonder of his sufficiency.

If you lack vision, having looked into the Word of God and waited upon the Spirit of God, look inside yourself; draw on your natural gifts and desires. Look at your calling. If you don't have one, you shouldn't be in leadership.

What has God called you to? When you know your calling and gifting, follow it and don't be diverted from it.

Specializing
The Lord Jesus Christ was a specialist. There is no doubt that he was appointed to a special task.

The Spirit of the Lord is on me,
because he has anointed me

to preach good news to the poor.
He has sent me to proclaim freedom for the prisoners
and recovery of sight for the blind,
to release the oppressed,
to proclaim the year of the Lord's favor.
Luke 4:18–19

The life of the Lord Jesus was unique. He was the Christ, God's anointed and appointed King. He came to earth to do what no one else could do. What is true of the Savior is true of his followers.

Ministry is a broad term. It includes every kind of service and like our Master our concern is for the whole person, physically, emotionally, socially and spiritually. Yet no one has been designed to meet all the needs of others. What must we do to keep focused? Does God's Word tell us? Yes, I believe it does, in Acts 6:1–7. Here we see how the apostolic leadership of the early church in Jerusalem faced a crisis and resolved it. Widows who had no other means of provision were cared for from a common purse. However, Jews who spoke mainly Greek (and may well have moved to Jerusalem from another country, leaving themselves cut off from family support) felt that they were being neglected in comparison to the locally born widows. We are not told how this happened but the apostles were concerned to put it right, although not at any cost. They realized that they must retain their ministry of prayer and communicating God's Word if the church was to remain healthy.

They also refused to impose a solution but suggested to the whole group that seven servant leaders should be appointed to share the work. The qualifications for the role were spelt out, involving both spiritual and practical matters. The group agreed with the idea, appointments were made and the church, renewed in health, continued to grow.

The early Christians were learning what Moses had to learn

about leadership from his father-in-law – delegate or die (Exodus 18.) More people had to be involved in different aspects of ministry and leadership if the church was to return to health and grow again.

It is interesting to note that 'the Twelve' committed themselves to 'give [their] attention to prayer and the ministry of the word'.

John Stott as always has a helpful comment:

It is vital for the health and growth of the church that pastors and people in the local congregation learn this lesson. True, pastors are not apostles, for the apostles were given authority to formulate and teach the gospel, while pastors are responsible to expound the message which the apostles have bequeathed to us in the New Testament. Nevertheless, it is a real 'ministry of the Word' to which pastors are called to dedicate their lives. The apostles were not too busy for ministry, but preoccupied with the wrong ministry. So are many pastors. Instead of concentrating on the ministry of the Word (which will include preaching to the congregation, counselling individuals and training groups) they have become overwhelmed with administration. Sometimes it is the pastor's fault (he wants to keep all the reins in his own hands), and sometimes the people's (they want him to be a general factotum). In either case the consequences are disastrous. The standards of preaching and teaching decline, since the pastor has little time to study or pray. And the lay people do not exercise their God-given roles, since the pastor does everything himself. For both reasons the congregation is inhibited from growing into maturity in Christ. What is needed is the basic, Biblical recognition that God calls different men and women to different ministries. Then the people will ensure that their pastor is set free from unnecessary administration, in order to give himself to the ministry of the Word, and the pastor will ensure that the people discover their gifts and develop ministries appropriate to them.[11]

I believe we must not ignore this reminder that leaders are to become specialists in prayer. This means that primarily we are to spend much time in prayer. Do you? Yes, we are to be busily engaged – in prayer. We are to be found often in prayer. Are you?

We need to see prayer as a ministry. That is to say we are to spend time in prayer not only for our own benefit but as a part of our spiritual preparation for ministry. We are also to intercede for our rulers in government, for laborers already at work in the 'harvest fields', for friends and colleagues, for our families and children. The spheres of our prayer concern ought to reach ever wider as we mature as spiritual leaders in the church, overcoming our own self-centeredness and losing ourselves in loving service to others.

Set your heart on becoming a specialist in the Word of God and in prayer. Pursue that goal; spend much time in the Word and prayer, always with the practical end in view that you may share what the Spirit teaches you. Here is the call to the expository preaching and teaching of scripture under the anointing of the Holy Spirit. Preach the Word in the power of the Spirit.

A dearth in these qualities of the Master among Christian leadership today causes the church to appear dead. The health of the church of Jesus Christ is dependent on anointed ministry. Be obedient to this calling and your church will be healthy and grow, spiritually and numerically. It will also determine the kind of epitaph that will be on your tombstone.

Chapter 6

'Dead Men Don't Eat Lunch'

Geoffrey Gilson, the author of *Dead Men Don't Eat Lunch*, is a natural storyteller and comic. He entertains with style and humor, as he gives the inside track on the scandals, brewing on both sides of the Atlantic, which will dramatically redefine the world's view of Margaret Thatcher, Tony Blair and both presidents Bush. Geoffrey is a writer, composer and radio broadcaster, who lives in North Carolina, USA. I use the title of his book to draw attention to another scandal: a church that is failing to feed the flock of Christ adequately. Spiritual malnutrition will cause churches to look more like skeletons than like the Body of Christ.

The year 1953 was an important time for our family. My dad bought our first television. It was a small set, showing only black and white pictures, but it seemed that the whole street crowded into our front room to watch the coronation of Queen Elizabeth II. I sat awestruck when the minister, whom I have since discovered was the Moderator of the General Assembly of the Church of Scotland, Dr Pitt Watson, handed the Bible to the newly crowned Queen, saying as he did so, 'Here is wisdom; this is the royal law; these are the lively oracles of God.'

Even as a ten-year old I was impressed. I had been raised in an evangelical home but I had never heard the Bible described in such a way. Wow, I thought, the Bible is given to the Queen to help her reign! And indeed it is. It should also be the means by which governments determine the laws that govern the land.

The Bible certainly should be the means whereby the church of Jesus Christ governs its affairs and Christians find guidance for life. Yet the majority of believers neglect the Word of God to their peril.

Pulling Out of the Nose Dive by Peter Brierley details the
results of the 2005 UK church census. Here are some statistics
about Bible reading in England: only 27% of churchgoers in
England in 2005 claimed to read the Bible personally at least once
a week, outside of church services. How does that work out
according to denominations?

Anglican	24%
Baptist	27%
Methodist	27%
Broad	42%
Pentecostal	62%
Independent	64%
New Church	66%

The larger the (Protestant) church (when the congregation
exceeds 300), the greater the proportion of members who read the
Bible. This finding is consistent with the research of any growing
church; you will discover that larger churches have this in
common: they have a high regard for the Word of God. Derek
Tidball, former Principal of the London School of Theology, has
written,

> The most characteristic feature of evangelicalism is the place it
> gives to the Bible. Its supreme symbol mid-20th century was
> Billy Graham, preaching to thousands, declaring, 'The Bible
> says...'. The backbone of the evangelical world is the multi-
> tudinous Bible schools and colleges. The quintessence of
> evangelical leisure is attendance at a Bible conference. The
> lifeblood of evangelical publishing is the Bible itself, or Bible
> commentaries. And much internal energy is consumed on
> debates about the Bible. Evangelicals see the Bible as the
> supreme authority for all matters concerning life and faith,

what they are to believe and how they are to behave. For them, 'It is the Bible, the whole Bible and nothing but the Bible.'[12]

A healthy church and healthy Christians enjoy a good diet of the Word of God. The Bible bears the stamp of divine authority, demonstrates life-giving vitality and is remarkable for its miraculous continuity. Let us unpack those words, authority, vitality and continuity, as they refer to the Bible.

The Bible's Divine Authority

We need to observe both the source and the force of the Bible's authority.

The source of the authority

For a source to be reliable it must be what the theologians call 'infallible'. And since we cannot believe anything the Bible says unless we believe what the Bible states about itself, we must take notice of that Word which declares, 'All Scripture is given by inspiration of God' (2 Timothy 3:16 New King James Version). While evangelical scholars are somewhat divided on the exegesis of these words, they are, generally speaking, agreed on the theological interpretation. By 'inspiration' is meant the supernatural activity of God on the human mind by which the prophets, the apostles and the sacred writers were qualified to spell out divine truth without any admixture of error. Needless to say, this definition of inspiration does not apply to the corruptions which have at times affected the translations of the text but rather to the scriptures as originally produced by the Breath of God.

Pick up your Bible and realize that in your hands you have authoritative documents which bear the very stamp of God's character and communication. We therefore can say with St Augustine, 'When the scriptures speak, God speaks.'

The force of the authority

Because of its infallible source, the Bible also carries an irresistible force. It is God's rule for us concerning all matters of faith and practice. This does not mean, of course, that the Bible teaches people such knowledge as they may obtain for themselves through patient study; on the contrary, the Bible is the revelation of truth which natural minds cannot research or understand. That is why Paul goes on to say, 'All Scripture is given by inspiration of God and is profitable for doctrine, for reproof, for correction, for instruction in righteousness, that the man of God may be complete, thoroughly equipped for every good work' (2 Timothy 3:16–17 NKJV). To understand the scriptures, we must know the in-dwelling and illumination of the Holy Spirit, for we are clearly told, 'The natural man does not receive the things of the Spirit of God, for they are foolishness to him; nor can he know them, because they are spiritually discerned. But he who is spiritual judges all things' (1 Corinthians 2:14–15 NKJV).

The Bible's Life-Giving Vitality

Having observed the authority of God's Word, the Bible, we now observe how the Word of God and the Spirit of God, when harnessed together, have a divine vitality.

Why is it that those churches that lay such emphasis on the Word of God and the Spirit of God grow? Let scripture speak for itself. For instance, creation came into being through the spoken word. 'God said, "'Let there be light'; and there was light' (Genesis 1:3 NKJV). This is confirmed by John's Gospel where we read,

In the beginning was the Word, and the Word was with God, and the Word was God. He was in the beginning with God. All things were made through him, and without him nothing was made that was made. In him was life, and that life was the

64

light of men.
John 1:1–4 NKJV

The writer to the Hebrews reminds us that 'the worlds were framed by the Word of God' (Hebrews 11:3 NKJV), and that he sustains 'all things by the word of His power' (Hebrews 1:3 NKJV). What an astonishing truth to realize that everything that lives and moves is pervaded by the generating and sustaining vitality which emanates from the out-going Word of God!

Scientists throughout the centuries have asked how the universe is held together. Only in recent years have they come to realize that there must be a central point of integration. Yet nearly 2,000 years ago, Paul could state that the Lord Jesus 'is before all things, and in him all things hold together' (Colossians 1:17). What power there is in the Word of God! When God speaks, universes come into existence.

This is why I am committed to expository preaching. As long as the anointing of the Spirit rests upon every utterance, I know the Word will do its work in the hearts of men and women.

Something happens when the Word of God is heard and mixed with faith. What a thrill it is to see an individual or a congregation develop in Christian character and conduct through the preaching of eternal truth! Those churches that are really alive and well are those whose pulpits have become sounding boards for the Word of God.

The Bible's Miraculous Continuity
Many people ask how a book completed almost 2,000 years ago can be relevant in the twenty-first century. The Bible says, 'The word of our God stands forever' (Isaiah 40:8). For us in the twenty-first century, this teaches three encouraging concepts.

The permanence of the Word of God
Someone has pointed out that if we stacked up all the volumes

ever written against the Bible, we could build a pyramid higher than the loftiest spire. For 2,000 years the enemies of the gospel have been firing away at scripture but making as much impression as they would shooting peas at the Rock of Gibraltar! For example, Voltaire declared that his writings would replace the Bible and that in 100 years it would be forgotten. God took up the challenge and 25 years later the very publishing house which published Voltaire's works became the center for the Geneva Bible Society!

Jesus said, 'Heaven and earth will pass away, but My words will by no means pass away' (Mark 13:31 NKJV). Men and movements may come and go but the Word of God stands for ever! Therefore a church solidly built on expository preaching will never crumble.

The relevance of the Word of God
Because of the permanence of the Bible it is always relevant. The Bible is always up to date in the light of contemporary history. It is divinely adapted to all countries, cultures and centuries. That is why preaching the Bible always meets the needs of spiritually hungry people. Things may satisfy the body, people may satisfy the soul, but only God can satisfy the spirit – that God-shaped hole that no one else but he can fill. That is why the diet of a healthy church must be the Holy Scriptures, understood with the help of the Holy Spirit.

The influence of the Word of God
The Bible is indispensable. It contains the only Word of the gospel for men and women. Within its covers we have an authoritative statement concerning the revelation of God and the redemption of humanity. While Christ is the final and authoritative revelation of God, the Bible is the final and authoritative revelation of Christ.

Every page of Holy Scripture focuses on Christ, for he is the central theme of the book. Only when we return to the Bible do we learn the name of Jesus by whom we find salvation. Through his death, burial and resurrection we can experience personal salvation. It is when we have met him personally that we realize that we need him to guide us by Word and by Spirit in matters touching the whole of our life.

The sanctity of married life, the security of family life and the stability of social life are linked to the moral and ethical standards taught in the Bible. Therefore we must allow the Word of Christ to 'dwell in [us] richly in all wisdom' (Colossians 3:16 NKJV). But the eternal influence of the Word of God ultimately affects the whole of life. No other book has a record of lives redeemed, moral outcasts regenerated, distressed souls cheered and nations remade. Never has the world known a higher code of ethics, nor has any book so influenced literature, language, art, music and education.

'Dead men don't eat lunch' but the church that feeds its people on a healthy diet of the Word will live and grow. Let us resolve to learn the Bible, love the Bible and live the Bible.

Even as I write, I can hear some saying, 'Amen!' It is at this very point that I want to challenge our real attitude to the Word of God. There are a few tests the Bible gives to us to help us gauge our appreciation for it.

• Would you rather have your Bible than you would food? Job said, 'I have treasured the words of his mouth more than my daily bread' (Job 23:12). God's Word is 'bread' (Matthew 4:4), 'milk and strong meat' (Hebrews 5:11–14 KJV) and even 'honey' (Psalm 119:103). Martha busied herself getting a meal but Mary chose to sit at the feet of a Master to be fed by his Word.

•Would you rather have God's Word than money? The psalmist had no doubt: 'The law from your mouth is more precious to me than thousands of pieces of silver and gold' (Psalm 119:72). A young man wrestling with his conscience about working on the Lord's Day chose to work although he knew that in doing so, he would miss out on worship. Little wonder that in no time at all he was backsliding.

• Would you rather have God's Word than sleep? Listen to the psalmist again: 'My eyes stay open through the watches of the night, that I may meditate on your promises' (Psalm 119:148). What a wonderful example that many need to follow! Some people cannot get to the morning meeting simply because they love their bed more than they love the Word.

It is one thing to claim we love the Word of God but it is another thing to show it. Our lives often deny it. We need to ensure that we not only attend worship services where the Bible is taught, and small groups where (among other things) the Bible is discussed, but that we read it in a systematic and devotional way.

People of my generation still talk of the 'quiet time'. Whatever you call it, such a time spent alone reading the Bible prayerfully and devotionally is vital to spiritual health, whether you are a newly converted or a mature Christian. Many people say they are too busy. But necessity is the mother of invention. Susanna Wesley, mother of John and Charles, with all the demands of home, family and church never missed a day of meeting the Lord in this way. She had no special room she could use so made a practice of pulling her apron over her head and shutting everyone out for that time.

One of my deacons was known every day, during his break time, to go into the company store room for his quiet time. We can do it when we want to.

However, there is an even greater test of our appreciation of the Word of God than this. The real test is whether or not we are willing to apply the Word of God to our lives; that is, to be not only hearers but also doers of the Word.

It is not enough to hear the Word of God; we must heed it. Many mistakenly believe that hearing a good message or doing a good Bible study is what helps us grow spiritually. It is not the hearing but the heeding of the Word that brings the blessing of God. Too many of us mark our Bibles but do not allow the Bible to mark us.

The Apostle James compared the Word of God to a mirror (James 1:22–25). A mirror allows us not only to examine ourselves but also to know what we need to do to correct what is not right. If we are to use God's mirror properly, we must examine our own hearts and lives in the light of God's Word. This requires time, attention and discipline. The Bible will reveal the will of God, but the blessing of God attends the doing of it.

The Word of God has in it the power to accomplish the Will of God. The Lord never asks us to anything he doesn't enable us to do. Jesus commanded the crippled man to stretch out his withered hand – the very thing he could not do. Yet the word of command gave him the power to obey. When we believe God's Word and obey it, he releases his power in us to fulfill his purpose.

Thank God too for the power of the Holy Spirit that accompanies the reading and the preaching of the Word of God. A clear illustration of this is found in the conversion of Cornelius, the Roman centurion, recorded for us in Acts chapter 10. Even before Peter had finished preaching the Word, the Holy Spirit began to fall on those who heard it. In verses 44 to 48 we have a description of life in the Spirit.

The Fruit of the Holy Spirit
We must never think that the diet of a healthy church consists of the Word alone. It is Word and Spirit. Every good meal goes down better with a good drink. We are to continue to drink deeply of God's Spirit. The coming of the Holy Spirit brings power to live. The fruit and the evidence of the Holy Spirit in a person's life is the production of love, joy, peace, patience, kindness, goodness, faithfulness, humility and self-control, and to know these qualities beyond the level possible for any

unredeemed person. The coming of Christ into a person's life by the power of the Holy Spirit brings the power to transform character and temperament – hallelujah!

The 'fruit of the Spirit' is the same as the character of the Lord Jesus. It is no accident that the Bible calls the third person of the Trinity the 'Holy' Spirit. One of the main functions of the Holy Spirit is to impart the holiness of God to us. He does this as he develops within us a Christ-like character, having a character marked by the 'fruit of the Spirit'. God's purpose is that we would 'become mature, attaining to the whole measure of the fullness of Christ' (Ephesians 4:13). God the Holy Spirit uses the word 'fruit' frequently in scripture to denote what he expects of his people in the way of character.

We must make a distinction between the 'gifts of the Spirit' and the 'fruit of the Spirit'. However, let it be said immediately that the two are not optional. Biblical Christianity should produce both. The fruit of the Spirit commences to grow immediately on conversion. The gifts may not be revealed straightaway. The fruit of the Spirit in all its varieties should be seen in every believer. All the gifts of the Spirit are not granted to every Christian. The fruit of the Spirit concerns qualities of disposition and temperament. The gifts of the Spirit involve activity.

The gifts of the Spirit are absolutely essential for the growth of the church but the gifts of the Spirit without the fruit of the Spirit are positively dangerous. It is for this reason that the two main chapters in Paul's first letter to the Corinthians which deal with the gifts of the Spirit (chapters 12 and 14) are sandwiched by his poem on love, which is the first of the fruits of the Spirit.

Unlike the gifts of the Spirit, the fruit of the Spirit is not divided among believers. Instead, all Christians should be marked by all the fruit of the Spirit. The fruit of the Spirit is God's expectation in our lives. This is clearly seen in many passages of scripture. In Matthew 13 Jesus told the familiar parable of the seed and the sower. He likens anyone declaring the Word of God, to a man sowing seed. And he is looking for a harvest. You and I are to bear fruit, as the Word of God begins to work in our lives in the power of the Spirit.

It is interesting that the Bible talks of the 'fruit' of the Spirit rather than the 'fruits'. A tree may bear many apples but all come from the same tree. In the same way, the Holy Spirit is the source of all fruit in our lives.

Put in simplest terms, the Bible tells us that we need the Spirit to bring fruit into our lives because we cannot produce godliness apart from the Spirit. In our own selves we are filled with all kinds of self-centered and self-seeking desires which are opposed to God's will for our lives. In other words, two things need to happen in our lives. First, the sin in our lives needs to be cut out. Secondly, the Holy Spirit needs to come in and fill our lives, producing the fruit of the Spirit.

The world needs the church of Jesus Christ to fulfill its potential and display supernatural and irresistible reality. Then they will know that the church is not dead.

Chapter 7

Take Off the Mask!

"The death mask of Egyptian pharaoh Tutankhamen is made of gold inlaid with colored glass and semiprecious stone. The mask comes from the innermost mummy case in the pharaoh's tomb, and stands 54 cm high and weighs around 11 kg.

The pharaoh is portrayed in a classical manner, with a ceremonial beard, a broad collar formed of 12 concentric rows consisting of inlays of turquoise, lapis lazuli, cornelian and amazonite. The traditional nemes head-dress has yellow stripes of solid gold broken by bands of glass paste, colored dark blue. On the forehead of the mask are a royal uraeus and a vulture's head, symbols of the two tutelary deities of Lower and Upper Egypt: Wadjet and Nekhbet. Above his perfect golden cheeks, Tutankhamen has blue petals of lapis lazuli in imitation of the kohl make-up he would have worn in life."[13]

Clearly, Tutankhamen's mask is a truly wonderful sight, but no matter how you wrap it up, it was used to cover dry bones! It is time for the masks to be removed from the Body of Christ so that its true identity might be revealed.

Larry Crabb writes:

The future of the church depends on whether it develops true community. We can get by for a while on size, skilled communication, and programs to meet every need, but unless we sense that we belong to each other, with masks off, the vibrant church of today will become the powerless church of tomorrow. Stale, irrelevant, a place of pretence where sufferers suffer alone, where pressure generates conformity rather than the Spirit creating life – that's where the church is headed unless it focuses on community.[14]

The coming of the Holy Spirit into the lives of the early Christians produced amongst them not only life in all its fullness but also a spirit of oneness in unity that excelled anything previously experienced by the people of God. So unique was the sense of community that the New Testament writers had to create a word to describe it, the word *koinonia*. Following the birthday of the church recorded for us in Acts chapter 2, we find that the early believers 'devoted themselves to…the fellowship'.

Unfortunately, like many other words in our language, 'fellowship' has become debased. The word has become so devalued that it seldom means more than a nice get-together in church, followed by coffee and biscuits! Fellowship is one of the great words of the New Testament and we need to redeem it and restore to it the meaning that was once attached to it.

Koinonia (from *koinos* – common) bears witness to the common life of the church in two senses. First, it expresses what we share in together. This is God himself, for 'our fellowship is with the Father and with his Son, Jesus Christ.' And there is 'the fellowship of the Holy Spirit'. Thus *koinonia* is a Trinitarian experience; it is our common share in God, Father, Son and Holy Spirit. But secondly *koinonia* also expresses what we share out together. What we give as well as what we receive. *Koinonia* is the word Paul used for the collection he was organising among the Greek churches, and *koinonikos* is the Greek word for 'generous'. It is to this Luke is particularly referring here, because he goes on at once to describe the way in which these first Christians shared their possessions with one another: 'All the believers were together and had everything in common (*koina*). Selling their possessions and goods (probably meaning their real estate and their valuables respectively), they gave to everyone as he had need.[15]

I am convinced that for a church to be a healthy congregation, it must discover once again the spirit of oneness and unity that marked the New Testament church. Is the degree of fellowship in your local church equal to that displayed by the early church in the Acts of the Apostles? If not, why not?

So often, we know the answer to that question. In our evangelism the greatest hindrance to the making of disciples is the reputation of the church.

The 'Peanuts' character Charlie Brown one day walked into an empty church and asked the telling question, 'Where are all the hypocrites gone?' The truth is that people are persuaded by the claims of Jesus Christ but when they look to the church they quickly become disillusioned. The central problem of the contemporary church is that it does not have enough of Christ in it to make it distinctive. In seeking to become culturally relevant, the church has become swamped by the world.

May God grant us a spirit of repentance for what we have allowed the church to become. It was said of the early church, 'See how they love one another', and since the beginning, healthy churches have been loving communities who demonstrate in their relationships the truth of the gospel.

Another unique word had to be created in the writing of the New Testament to describe the love which God demonstrated to us in Christ – *agape*. The Greek term *agape* has a special meaning. It is not primarily an emotion but a determination of the will always to seek what is best for others, no matter how they treat us. It is showing a willingness to 'prefer' one another and to sacrifice for the sake of one another in relationships. It is demonstrated by a willingness to lay down one's personal agenda. A healthy church is therefore one characterized by honesty, openness, mutual supportiveness and pastoral care.

John Stott, in the quotation just mentioned, refers to two

aspects of *koinonia* – the 'sharing in' and the 'sharing out'.

Sharing In
Let us unpack those two thoughts. First, *koinonia* expresses what we 'share in' together. We are partners with God and with each other and shareholders in eternity. We share a common inheritance – the Christian faith. The same God who lives in me lives in you. The same blood that cleansed me cleansed you. The same Spirit who energizes my life energizes you. It is this being in Christ, and having Christ in us, that makes us one.

There is no other movement, organization or society on earth in which you will find that same level of partnership as in a healthy church. I had the joy recently of receiving into membership at the same time a refuse collector and a doctor. In another service I baptized a 17-year-old, a 35-year-old and a 75-year-old. We all come into the Christian church through the same door, that door being Christ. All distinctions are leveled and all that is given to us is by grace and not through human effort. This produces in us a sense of fellowship which is unique and distinctive.

I have always longed to have a multicultural congregation. As the movement of people across the continents increases, we might expect it more and more. 'There is neither Jew nor Greek, slave nor free, male nor female, for you are all one in Christ Jesus' (Galatians 3:28).

I am well aware of the stupidities, hypocrisies and failures of the church but there is flowing through the church a common life, a common bond, a common energy, that if we flow with it lifts us above every difference into a celebration of the oneness we have in Christ.

The need to belong
The truth is that the search for such a community is a fundamental life search. We all need to belong but I believe it used to

be easier to belong to the church than it is today. I was raised in a zealous evangelical family, so there is a sense in which I have always belonged to the church. I cannot remember a time when I didn't believe in Christ; having professed faith at age 11, I was baptized as a believer when 12 years old and became a member of the church. I believed, therefore I belonged. Today it is so different, living in a culture that values belonging over believing.

The telephone rang. It was Richard asking me if I would visit him as soon as possible. I gladly consented because his parents had been members of our church and during the past year both of them had passed away. Richard had only come to Tabernacle for the funeral services. He was a 'loner', a very deep-thinking person who expressed himself through the arts. He did not find 'community' an easy experience. He went to work at the same job and came home to the same place for years but never had any friends at work. He had people he visited, friends of his parents. There was just one group he belonged to, where his artistic ability was valued. His invitation to me to go and see him was something I had prayed for so much. I wanted him to feel he belonged to the fellowship.

I managed to see Richard later that day. He handed me an envelope, a copy of his last will and testament. 'Open it', he said.

He had made the church a major beneficiary. 'Why such generosity to Tabernacle?' I asked.

With a note of surprise he replied, 'Why, it's my church! Through the care you've shown to my parents, you've made me feel I belong.'

Does Richard belong to our fellowship? You won't find his name on the membership list but we have created a special category: 'Friends of Tabernacle'. Richard belongs because he feels that he belongs. No, he is not a disciple but he belongs. About six months after our conversation, he turned up at a worship service. He was made to feel welcome and after the service he explained to me it was a special date. Naturally I took the opportunity to say he would be welcome at any time. We invited him to the Alpha Course and to belong to a small group but as yet he is just 'a friend of Tabernacle'.

Joseph Myers defines belonging in the following terms:

> Belonging happens when you identify with another entity – a person or organization, or perhaps a species, culture, or ethnic group. Belonging need not be reciprocal. You can feel a sense of belonging – and in fact can belong – without the other party's knowledge or sharing the experience.[16]

Richard's case illustrates that belonging is an individual experience. He did not need my permission to belong in a significant way. Here is the distinction between *agape* and *koinonia*. *Agape* is the unconditional love of God for sinners. It is the benchmark of our love for others. In committing ourselves to be a loving community, we commit ourselves to being an inclusive community. The church is called to be like Jesus in his welcoming attitude to everyone. There is no doubt that the tax collector, the prostitute and every other social outcast was made to feel by Jesus that he loved them, valued them and included them in the scope of his care.

Of course, Jesus set out the demands of discipleship: 'If anyone would come after me, he must deny himself and take up his cross and follow me.' It is those who are prepared to meet the demands of discipleship that can enter into the full joy of *koinonia* – the fellowship.

The challenge for the church is to hold these two glorious words and concepts, *agape* and *koinonia*, in harmony.

Sharing Out
We have been reflecting on the idea implicit in *koinonia*: the expressing of what we share in together. Christian fellowship is our common share in God's great salvation. However, fellowship

is more than sharing in; it also involves a 'sharing out'. *Koinonia* not only concerns what we possess but what we do with what we possess.

It is because of what we have discovered in Christ that we want to share it with others. A study of Acts 2:42–47 outlines some of the evidences of true Christian fellowship:

> They devoted themselves to the apostles' teaching and to the fellowship, to the breaking of bread and to prayer. Everyone was filled with awe, and many wonders and miraculous signs were done by the apostles. All the believers were together and had everything in common. Selling their possessions and goods, they gave to anyone as he had need. Every day they continued to meet together in the temple courts. They broke bread in their homes and ate together with glad and sincere hearts, praising God and enjoying the favor of all the people. And the Lord added to their number daily those who were being saved.

What a picture of oneness, joyfulness and usefulness! However strongly some may dismiss this as a short-lived experiment, occasioned by the phenomenal number of new disciples at that time in Jerusalem, it cannot be denied that the whole pattern of shared life and love was created and controlled by the Holy Spirit. And since the Holy Spirit is still with us, surely the same evidences of fellowship should continue among us. Indeed a careful comparison makes it quite clear that the varied expression of social life, as described here, is merely the outworking of the 'Sermon on the Mount'.

The Sermon on the Mount is recorded for us in Matthew's Gospel and covers three chapters: 5 through to 7. It is important to note that this teaching was given first to the disciples. In most churches when a minister is ordained, there is an ordination service laying out the principles of life for the minister. This teaching of Jesus was like an ordination address to the first disciples and, beyond them, it was the commission for every Christian, setting out as it does the principles to govern the way we live and work. The Sermon on the Mount is the pattern of our life for those who have received the Lord Jesus as Savior.

What is more, Jesus reveals his method of winning the world; it is through the lives of those who have received him. Jesus intends that the people of the world should be won through the church, as Christians demonstrate the life of Christ among them.

Victor Hugo's *Les Misérables* tells the story of a village whose inhabitants have been robbed. The local bishop goes to visit the thieves in their hideout. The people don't want the bishop to endanger his life but he goes laughing, knowing that the worst the robbers could do to him is kill him – and then he would be with Christ! We do not know what happened to the bishop but we do know that the next day the villagers got back most of the stolen items.

Our Lord understood the power of such a life and he was setting out the principles for changed human lives and the Kingdom of God on earth. What we read in the Acts of the Apostles is the Spirit-inspired efforts of the early Christians to be true to those principles.

• 'All the believers were together and had everything in common' (Acts 2:44). Let us not underestimate the power of unity. It matters to God; it should matter to us. 'How good and pleasant it is when brothers live together in unity!' (Psalm 133:1). The clause 'when brothers live together in unity' has a close parallel in Deuteronomy 25:5 where it refers to an extended family living in close quarters. Some have therefore seen this psalm as a plea to restore or preserve this social pattern. Such unity never exclaims about an item of personal possession, 'That's mine!' but says rather, 'If you need it, it's yours.'

• 'Selling their possessions and goods, they gave to anyone as he had need' (Acts 2:45). No one could be called needy as long as the spirit of fellowship functioned. How we work that out in practice will vary from congregation to congregation, but face the challenge of it we must. It never ceased to amaze me the way the fellowship at Tabernacle worked this out. A young couple on the fringe of the fellowship lost almost everything due to a kitchen fire. One of our leaders phoned me and made me aware of the situation. Not only was overnight accommodation provided by another family, but within 24 hours their flat had been redecorated and refurbished, all by people from within our local fellowship. I could tell that story over and over again. Every time we plan a church weekend away from the area, there are always some people who cannot afford the price of the trip. The notice is always given: 'If you believe that the Lord wants you to go and you cannot afford it, put your name down and speak to one of the pastors.' The name of the person who isn't paying is never publicized, but you can always be sure that someone who is able will pay for them to go.

Often the evidence of the Holy Spirit's involvement is clear. Needs are not always admitted but people find themselves prompted by the Holy Spirit to give, and this is often met by the testimony, 'That gift came just at the right time.'

The Spirit of *agape* and *koinonia* is alive and well but we must make it work in our local congregations.

• 'Every day they continued to meet together in the temple courts. They broke bread in their homes and ate together with glad and sincere hearts' (Acts 2:46). There was faithfulness in their love and in their gathering for fellowship. Sometimes we need to encourage one another back into fellowship. 'Let us not give up meeting together, as some are in the habit of doing, but let us encourage one another – and all the more as you see the Day approaching' (Hebrews 10:25).

Healthy churches seek to work out these principles in the local congregation. They are not perfect and are aware of the forces at work to spoil their best efforts but they stick to the task.

In practical terms how can we pursue this kind of loving within the church? There are a number of biblical principles which, if practiced, will help you to grow in love and fellowship.

Respect and Honor One Another
On becoming Christians, we see people differently. Paul put it like this: 'So from now on we regard no-one from a worldly point of view. Though we once regarded Christ in this way, we do so no longer. Therefore if anyone is in Christ, he is a new creation; the old has gone, the new has come!' (2 Corinthians 5:16–17). We look at one another through the eyes of Jesus. We no longer want to stand in judgment, criticizing and finding fault. As God deals with us, so we begin to deal with one another. We no longer need to compete with others or get one over on them. Instead we want to put others before ourselves. This is the change of attitude that Jesus brings about. It is particularly hard for someone like me with a dominating personality. The transformation in me has been slow. It is one of those areas I have to concentrate on. The trouble is that when anyone tries to dominate a group, they are demonstrating they are not honoring others above themselves. It is also fatal, for when we try to dominate others they try to dominate us and then the stage is set for clash and strife.

Seek to Serve One Another
One of the most amazing occasions in the life of Jesus is recorded for us in John 13. During the Last Supper on the evening of his arrest, Jesus took a towel and washed his disciples' feet. This was the work of a slave. There was no one else at that meal that would have been prepared to carry out this task – they were too proud. But Jesus set them an example and said, 'Now that I, your Lord and Teacher, have washed you feet, you also should wash one another's feet' (John 13:14). We should all be seeking oppor-tunities to serve our sisters and brothers with a humble heart. We should not despise the fulfilling of menial and unpleasant tasks

for the sake of God's people; instead we should actively seek them.

Forgive One Another

We owe a lot to Simon Peter. He often 'put his foot in it', saying things which not only prompted Jesus to put him right but also ensured that a lesson was recorded for us all to learn. On one occasion Peter came to the Lord Jesus and asked how often he ought to forgive his brother; he then answered his own question by suggesting that he should forgive seven times. In saying this, Peter thought he was being very generous. It was the teaching of the rabbis that a man should forgive his brother three times. So Peter was doubling it and adding a bit more for good measure. Peter expected to be warmly commended and could never have guessed what Jesus was going to say: 'Seventy times seven'. Then Jesus told the story of a servant forgiven a huge debt who then went out and dealt without mercy with a colleague who owed him a much smaller amount. The servant expected to be forgiven but refused to forgive his colleague. We learn from the teaching of Jesus that his Father regards any refusal to forgive with great seriousness. How can those who have been forgiven so much refuse to forgive others? When we consider the sufferings of our Lord Jesus Christ – his death upon the cross so that he might forgive those who come to him in faith – how, in the light of that, can we refuse to extend forgiveness to others?

I do not think there is a more important lesson for the church in any age to learn than this. If the church is to be healthy there must be harmony and if there is to be harmony in a church then Christians will need to learn how to be gracious, as God is gracious. God's children can only live in love and harmony if they are prepared to be gracious with one another.

Reconciliation dynamic

So important is this principle that Jesus gives a step-by-step procedure if there is a breakdown in relationships. We find it in Matthew 18:15–20: 'If your brother sins against you, go and show him his fault... If he listens to you, you have won your brother over.' That is quite clear. The responsibility for taking action over a broken relationship always lies with you. This is true not only if a person sins against you but when you sin against someone else. Going to someone whom you have hurt, or who has hurt you, has been and always will be the greatest test of genuine love.

Our motivation needs to be checked out first. It must not be for the sake of confrontation but of reconciliation. There also needs to be a time of sincere heart-searching before we make any move towards someone with whom we have fallen out.

However, having searched our own heart and checked our motivation we have to go. What are the steps?

1. Discuss the matter confidentially with the person concerned. Do not discuss it with anyone before you discuss it with the person concerned. This first step, when acting out of a spirit of love and reconciliation, nearly always works. If we have been wronged then it is extremely unusual for this approach not to result in an apology and reconciliation.

However, if it does not work then notice the next step.

2. 'But if he will not listen, take one or two others along so that "every matter may be established by the testimony of two or three witnesses".' The presence of one or two other people indicates the seriousness of the situation. It is always best to ensure that the person or people you take with you will be acceptable to the other party and considered fair-minded and objective.

If this step is not successful then the Lord Jesus tells us what to do.

3. 'If he refuses to listen to them, tell it to the church; and if he refuses to listen even to the church, treat him as you would a pagan or a tax collector.' This is when you take the breakdown in

relationships to the local church. Most people understand this to mean the leaders of the church. However, it is extremely unusual to have to go as far as this. Here again it must be seen that the purpose of sharing the problem with the leaders of the church is not to expose but to restore.

Watch the Tongue

The Bible recognizes the power of the human tongue. It is one of the smaller parts of the human body but it has great power. 'All kinds of animals, birds, reptiles and creatures of the sea are being tamed and have been tamed by man, but no man can tame the tongue. It is a restless evil, full of deadly poison' (James 3:7–8). We really do have to find an answer to the evil tongue that sometimes demonstrates itself in the Body of Christ.

I want to commend a principle and a policy, which, if adopted, can address this matter, and eliminate all forms of gossip, backbiting and disharmony in a congregation.

The policy I am referring to is described as 'giving a good report'. The concept was first devised by an American Bible teacher, Bill Gothard, after a close examination of Matthew 18. It was popularized by Selwyn Hughes when he referred to it in the ever popular publication *Every Day With Jesus* in May–June 1982. Our church was so taken with it that in the following year we adopted it as a major goal for 1983 – with amazing results. We entered a period when we grew more quickly than at any other time. The effects lasted for a number of years before we had to return to it and reinforce the principle and the policy.

The policy is based on the text before us today. 'Pleasant sights and good reports give happiness and health.' Proverbs 15:30. It works like this – each member of a fellowship makes a commitment to give only a good report of others, and never to give a bad report unless they have first been to the person concerned and followed the principles we have just considered laid down in Matthew 18. The policy is not a vow, but simply a statement of intent. The value of such a commitment is that it establishes a course of action in ones mind to be free of indecision and to become more creative in finding ways to do what has already been established as a principle. As one member of the fellowship said, when this policy was introduced, 'It gives me a marvellous feeling to know that no one would give a bad report about me before checking with me first.'[17]

Committing yourself to this should not be regarded as a vow because human nature being what it is, and remembering that the tongue is the most difficult member to tame, there will be times when you will break the commitment. When you do break it, and give a bad report of someone, first ask God's forgiveness, then go to the one you have offended and ask their forgiveness. You will discover, if you follow this procedure, that after a while the urge to give a bad report of someone, which stems from the carnal nature, will be overcome by the pain and challenge of having to ask forgiveness.[18]

At this stage the question must be considered: What is a bad report? It is using words that put someone else in a bad light. It is damaging someone else's reputation with information that does not need sharing. It is encouraging or spreading discontent, gossip or discord among others. It is possible, of course, to give a bad report of someone without using words – by gestures, facial expressions or tone of voice. Actually we can say more through negative facial expressions and gestures than we can through our words. As Christians we must keep a constant check, not only on the words we speak, but also on our tone of voice, expressions and physical gestures. What a revolution would take place in our churches and fellowships if we all committed ourselves to giving only good reports!

Selwyn Hughes then dealt with two questions which might

arise in the minds of some about committing ourselves to giving a good report of everyone and never indulging in bad reports.

One question might be: What if I am required to give a recommendation for someone which will be negative? In this case discuss it with the person concerned and share with them the things you feel would hinder you giving a good report of their work. Encourage them by saying that their willingness to work on those areas would be the framework in which you would give your report.

Another question that might come to mind is this: How do I stop someone giving a bad report about someone else to me? As soon as you realise that someone is giving you a bad report about another person, stop them and say: 'Are you telling me this so that I might be a witness in restoring this person according to Matthew 18?' If not then lovingly suggest that as you are not directly involved (if this should be the case) then you prefer not to hear it. If someone persists in wanting to share with you a negative report about someone else then follow the scriptural principle in Proverbs 25:23 which explains that as the North wind drives away rain, so aggrieved countenance drives away a backbiting tongue. Show your disapproval by aggrieved countenance.

Other questions will undoubtedly spring to mind but if you keep before you the principle that, 'As a Christian, your main motivation is always to restore and not to revile', then you will find yourself dealing with any unanswered questions in a right way. Get the principle right, the policy will follow of its own accord.[19]

Would you consider committing yourself to being one who endeavors to give only a good report of others? Below is one form that is used by thousands of Christians. Ponder it carefully and if you feel you can sign it, do so.

Giving a Good Report

In obedience to the Word of God, I hereby commit myself to the goal of giving a good report. When this is not possible, I shall remain silent or go privately to the person concerned and explain the offence or problem preventing me giving a good report of them. I propose to approach an offender in a spirit of genuine love, having first examined and corrected my own attitudes and actions. Only if I am unable to restore an offender will I share the problem with others, according to the principles of scripture. When I violate this goal, I shall ask forgiveness, knowing that God resists the proud but gives grace to the humble.

Signed:...

I actually signed that statement on 29 June 1982 with a little prayer written alongside it: 'Lord, give me grace!'

As mentioned, our church adopted this policy in 1983 with amazing consequences. I can honestly say that ever since, I have, by the grace of God, been faithful to that statement of intent. I find myself practicing it almost every week. I pray that God might cause this simple principle and policy to have the same effect in your life and fellowship as it has in mine.

It is vital that we affirm our belief that the church of Jesus Christ is called to be different. It is called to be a loving, accepting, forgiving, gracious community in which the Christian can be securely and lovingly nurtured and where those who want to belong, but are not yet ready to believe, may feel part of the community.

This is an enormous challenge but let's not shrink from it. As we walk close to Christ, we can walk humbly and lovingly with one another. It is time to take off the masks.

One of the best ways of making *koinonia* work is creating small groups and that is what we will discuss next.

Chapter 8

To Cell or Not To Cell?

By the time a human being reaches adulthood, the body consists of close to 100 trillion cells. Each is part of an organ system designed to perform essential life functions. The biological cell is a basic building-block of life. Healthy cells multiply millions of times in the course of a lifetime. Each new cell looks identical to the original cell because the DNA-branded nucleus multiplies itself before the cell reproduces. In this way, the first cell is as healthy and productive as the newest cell formed. The cells work together as organs, muscles, bone and skin to make the body function as a true miracle from God.

A spiritual cell group is very similar to a biological cell. Followers of Jesus Christ, members of the Body of Christ, worship together, edify one another and increase the Kingdom by sharing their lives with unbelievers. New leaders are raised up from within the group to grow and expand the ministry to a hurting world when the group multiples, and the process repeats itself.

To understand more of this latest development in the use of small groups in the church you could visit www.celluk.org.uk where questions are answered and contact is welcomed. The Internet has similar websites for other countries around the world.

Cell groups meet weekly in homes and come together with other cells as a local body at celebration services. Both gatherings are vital! The cell meets to experience Christ's love through others in a small, intimate setting. The celebration service is to experience God in corporate worship and to receive teaching from his Word. Both are necessary for God's people to be empowered and encouraged into a sense of destiny and purpose in what they do from Monday to Friday.

Each cell is based around the following beliefs and values:

- Jesus is at the center of the gathered believers and the individual Christian's life.
- Christian community is fostered through relationship.
- Each member can grow in their Christian walk and knowledge of God.
- Every member can be released to minister to others in the Body of Christ.
- Every member can seek to bring others to Christ.

There is, however, a divergence of opinion on the place of small groups in the local church. Some believe the 'cell' church is the best thing since sliced bread. Others are fearful of the effects small groups can have, and still others are frustrated because they feel they have been there, done that and worn the T-shirt, but *koinonia* has not been experienced.

Freedom to Choose
In my view, it is not a matter of being for or against small groups but allowing Christians the freedom to choose the best way to fulfill their calling to be a disciple.

Gerald is a senior civil servant and a mature Christian who feels his primary ministry and mission must be his place of work. It is where he spends most of his waking hours. Gerald is not part of the fellowship group network of the church. However, he is responsible for running the Christian Fellowship in his government department, and the people in this group, who meet at least once a week during their lunchtime, are in a committed relationship. With all the demands of discipleship as it relates to being a husband, father, grandfather, responsible church member and senior civil servant, Gerald needs supporting, not pressurizing to join another small group.

Stephen is a senior manager and has to spend two or three nights away from home every week. There is no doubting his commitment to Christ and the church but he cannot commit himself to being in a small group. However, he is not missing out on belonging or community. He belongs to a group of men, not an organized group but a circle of male friends who are under the same pressures to balance the demands of life, home, work and worship. They meet as often as they can for a social evening which always includes a time of discussion around a biblical theme and a time of prayer.

I am absolutely committed to small groups as a vital part of a healthy church. However, I do not believe that fellowship groups (or whatever you call them) are necessarily the solution to the individual's search to belong.

We could add several other groupings of people to the list of those who find it difficult to belong to a fellowship group, including the housebound, those who have responsibility for caring for the housebound, and some single parents. Though difficult, joining is not impossible if the wider church has the capacity and capability of arranging support, enabling those who find it difficult to attend to do so. We assign all such people to groups and include them in the total sphere of activities as and when they can be involved.

The challenge of the local church in pastoral care is to ensure that all members of the community are cared for and developed in a way acceptable to them.

Pastoral Care

In my opinion, every disciple should be encouraged and assisted to belong to an appropriate small group. There are plenty of options. Some groups can be held during the day, morning and afternoon, and some in the evening. Some can be specifically youth groups, some for older people, others for a mixed age range. Some people are put into a certain group because they can handle a heavier diet, the 'meat' of the Word, while others are helped to develop with a less demanding diet.

It is the shepherd's responsibility to ensure that the sheep are protected, cared for and fed appropriately. However, unlike sheep, people can make choices and disciples need to be helped to make the right choices. At the end of the day, each individual must choose.

In our church a leader is appointed to oversee the pastoral caring scheme. In an attempt to develop a real sense of community, this scheme is based on small groups, the leaders of which are mainly responsible for the care of the people allocated to them. Practically, however, the members of the group 'care' for one another, including their leaders, of course. Those unable to join a small group, for whatever reason, are appointed a pastoral carer who seeks to maintain vital contact with and to support them whenever and wherever necessary.

As in all matters relating to health and well-being it is a matter of harmony or balance. David Beer writes:

Small groups are an essential part of a healthy church. Build the same balance into each small group that is being built into the church as a whole. Whatever the size of the church, small groups are where God's purposes for the church can be applied and practiced. They strengthen the whole of the church... They will be a place of fellowship, belonging and pastoral care. Each group will be a place for worship. Share communion together if you can do so within the parameters set by your denomination. The small group is also a place for serving one another (ministry), and a place of teaching (discipleship). Make each group inclusive and not exclusive, welcoming new people (mission), and find purpose champions: a worship champion, ensuring that the group does worship together at appropriate times; a fellowship champion, ensuring that there are authentic connections; a discipleship champion, ensuring that there is a systematic teaching schedule; a mission champion, bringing to the attention of the group matters of mission, both locally and world-wide; and a ministry champion, ensuring that serving one anther is a feature of the group and the group might corporately serve in the ministry together.[20]

David Beer, until he died, led a movement of churches called The Purpose Driven Churches of the United Kingdom. Every church he led grew – and grew dramatically. His voice needs to be heard by those seriously considering the well-being of the local church.

One of the most thrilling moments in reading David Beer's book was when I came to the testimonies of two older men that I've admired throughout my ministry. Maurice Rowlandson, who for 26 years was head of the Billy Graham Evangelistic Association in the UK, greatly surprised his friends when after a lifetime of resisting small groups he joined one. He now testifies that only by sharing in a small group has he learnt to derive the fullest benefit from belonging to the fellowship.

The other testimony came from Rev. Norman Wright, a former President of the Baptist Union of Great Britain. Having retired after 50 years in the Baptist ministry, always suspicious and doubtful about the value of small groups, he has now joined one at the church where he is a member.

> Immediately I was made welcome and played my part in the group, where I felt very much at home. The large church suddenly became very personal. I know that in reality nothing becomes significant or powerful until it becomes personal... After 48 years I finally joined a small group and realized what I had been missing.[21]

I so relate to those testimonies. I too was raised with a whole list of reasons why creating small groups in churches is not a good idea. In the past 20 years of ministry I have seen all of those myths exploded.

Christian Schwarz says:

If we were to identify any one principle as the 'most important', then without a doubt it would be the multiplication of small groups. In order to give proper weight to the strategic importance of small groups, we have conceptualised nearly all our church growth materials so that they can be used in small group context.[22]

Function of Groups

In order to understand the true nature of *koinonia* we need to understand the function of a small group. Unless we can produce this kind of fellowship in a small group, we will never produce it in a large group.

Clearly this approach is biblical. In the New Testament the Christians, having been thrown out of the temples and synagogues, evidently met in homes, usually as small groups of people. For instance, look at Romans 16:3-5: 'Greet Priscilla and Aquila, my fellow-workers in Christ Jesus… Greet also the church that meets at their house.' And again Paul sends his greetings 'to Apphia our sister, to Archippus our fellow-soldier and to the church that meets in your home' (Philemon 1:2). They obviously met in large groups from time to time but their spiritual growth and development took place in homes.

But what form should small groups take? Let us listen to David Beer again:

To enable every person to have a voice, a small group needs to have between 12 and 15 people. Finding leaders is not easy, but it is sometimes made easier if the responsibilities of leading the group are shared. For example, the person who hosts the group need not be the person who teaches the group. The role of teaching can be shared. Some churches are not prepared to take this risk, but future leaders have to be grown and they will make mistakes. All too often churches are looking for ready-made teachers and leaders rather than those who have the potential for leading and gifts that need to be developed through practice. Ask every group leader to identify a deputy leader who could be trained to lead a group. Again, use this group as a leadership factory.[23]

I inherited a number of small 'growth groups' (as they were called in 1982) and I was soon convinced of their value. They have been renamed since and have redefined their purpose.

What is a Cell Meeting Like?
Each cell meeting has a structure within it which enables the cell leader to be a facilitator leader. A typical cell meeting could comprise the following four elements – known as the 'four Ws'.

• Welcome. An 'icebreaker' question is asked of every cell member, who in turn all give their response. Each member thus participates from the outset, hears their own voice in the meeting and feels included from the start rather than spectating.

• Worship. This could be sung worship if there are musicians in the group. If not, it could be anything that exalts the Lord in the meeting, for example the reading of a psalm followed by a pause for reflection and prayer.

• Word. This section is based around personal application of a teaching, perhaps from the Sunday service or other source. Often at this point there will be opportunity for corporate prayer for those who request it – an opportunity for the cell members to minister to one another.

• Witness. Based around the corporate aim of making friends with non-believers and seeing them come to Christ, this section is often used for planning strategy and prayer.

Training and Equipping

We developed our own Leadership Training Course that equipped leaders and potential leaders so that when the need for new leaders arose, people were prepared for the role.

The small group leaders network together, not only for training but for communication. Usually leaders of small groups meet once every three months to reflect on the past session and to plan for the next. You can also plan ways in which the groups need to be developed and the movement of members from one group to another.

Consistently over the years, it has been the testimony of those that belong to small groups that they feel well cared for, whereas those who for one reason or another do not belong to a committed small group often feel that their needs are not being adequately met.

No church will ever succeed in getting everyone into a small group but this should not be considered as failure. The leadership of a healthy congregation will be aware of the temperament differences of those they care for. The truth is that no one but the Lord himself can meet our deep desire to belong. A person's search for community is more complex than this. People can experience a sense of belonging in groups ranging in size from two to 2,000 or more. As an advocate for small groups as a major key to a healthy congregation, I recognize that they are not the panacea for all ills.

However, I am convinced that the church, as a 'hospital' made up of sinners saved by grace, is better served by having small wards where specialist needs can be attended to in more personal ways.

It is the destiny of every Christian to be a part of the fellowship, the *koinonia*, and the only thing that can stop it is our unwillingness to be a part of it. One thing is sure: the church is only healthy to the degree that it can and does produce *koinonia*.

Tabernacle, Penarth is still transitioning from a church

committed to having fellowship groups to a church where these small groups are at the core of its purpose. My successor as senior pastor, Rev. Roger Grafton, is leading the church towards this purpose. Our understanding about the transition necessary has been greatly helped by William Beckham's book, *The Second Reformation: Reshaping the Church for the 21st Century*, which is an informed, sustained argument for the New Testament pattern of large-group celebration with small-group discipleship. *The Second Reformation* lovingly, yet firmly, challenges us to evaluate the church today. This book deals with hard questions many of us have wrestled with for years:

- Why is the church so ineffective at confronting the desperate needs of our society?
- Why are so many church leaders experiencing burnout?
- How do we shift from just making converts to making disciples?
- Can we really experience the church we read about in the book of Acts?

Not satisfied with simply pointing to problems in the church, Beckham also suggests biblical and practical solutions to these problems. After assessing the current state of the church, he lays a firm theological foundation before outlining a practical design for the twenty-first-century church. With years of experience as a pastor, missionary, church planter and teacher, he challenges the church to evaluate its beliefs and design against our sole source of authority, the Bible.

Two-Winged Church

Beckham describes the two-winged church:

The Creator once created a church with two wings; one wing was for large-group celebration, the other wing was for small-group community. Using both wings, the church could soar high into the heavens, enter into his presence and do his will over all the earth.

After a hundred years of flying across the earth, the two-winged church began to question the need for the small-group being. The jealous, wicked serpent who had no wings, loudly applauded this idea. Over the years, the small-group wing became weaker and weaker from lack of exercise until it virtually had no strength at all. The two-winged church that had soared high in the heavens was now for all practical purposes one-winged.

The Creator of the church was very sad. He knew the two-winged design had allowed the church to soar into his presence and do his bidding. Now with only one wing, just lifting off the ground required tremendous energy and effort. If the church did manage to become airborne, it was prone to flying in circles, lose its sense of direction, and not fly very far from its take-off point. Spending more and more time in the safety and comfort of its habitat, it grew contented with an earth-bound existence.

From time to time, the church dreamed of flying into the presence of the Creator, and doing his work all over the earth. But now, the strong large-group being controlled every movement of the church and doomed it to an earth-bound existence.

In comparison, the Creator finally stretched forth his hand and re-shaped his church so it could use both wings. Once again the Creator possessed a church that could fly into his presence and soar high over all the earth, fulfilling his purposes and plans.[24]

I commend Beckham's book to all who are considering making the transition, putting small groups back at the heart of seeking to create *koinonia*.

How to Group

I have already indicated my preference for a rainbow-colored church, a local church made up of every strand of society, every race, every language, every culture, every educational level, and every economic bracket. However, when it comes to small groups there is real wisdom in developing them in homogenous units.

Ideally, small groups are formed by dividing people into groups roughly according to where they live. Every newcomer is treated as an individual, suggestions are made and choices offered. There can be special interest groups, whose members naturally belong together. You may recall my reference to youth groups and those for senior citizens. They consist of people who have something in common and are therefore likely to have some common problems – issues that might not be of as much interest to other people in the church. The groups may or may not follow a common theme, but themes will certainly be applied by the group in a way that is appropriate to them.

There is an exciting development amongst teenage small groups. Teens have special problems but so do people in their twenties, thirties, forties and so on, right through life. This of course is only relevant to those churches which are attracting large numbers of people in every age bracket. However, there are some young people and some old people that want to be in a mixed-age group to learn from each other. That is excellent and should be encouraged.

For what Purpose?

Although transitioning to a 'cell' church, there is good reason to maintain the name 'fellowship group', not least because we need to keep the idea of *koinonia* alive. I believe that the principal purpose for a small group is to develop fellowship and this is probably the most difficult aspect to develop. If we are to come to maturity as Christians, as a community we should know one another, love one another and take an interest in one another's lives.

An important part of every meeting should be the sharing in a spirit of honesty and openness. If anyone is hurting they should be encouraged to share their hurt. It is important that all barriers are taken down and all masks removed. People come into a group with many barriers: fears, anxieties, resentments, inhibitions, unrest, guilt, self-centeredness and so on. There are of course dangers in encouraging this kind of openness and it needs a wise leader to preside. Some things ought not to be shared and leaders must be brave in what they allow and what they don't allow to be communicated. For instance gossip or negative reports must not be shared.

For a group to reach this stage of sharing is to reach a pinnacle. When a group is first formed, there will be a reluctance to open up in this way. Once again, leaders have a key role to play in knowing how much to share of themselves. When you want to encourage someone else to open up to you, you set the example, sharing some of your own anxieties, fears and inhibitions. When we open up to each other, we find we carry the same openness into our relationship with God. And the more open we are to him, the more of himself he can pour into us.

This leads quite correctly into the second purpose of a fellowship group. It is to pray together. Often the prayers will flow from the sharing. Once again the 'prayer leader' of a group has a great responsibility here to encourage praise, thanksgiving, confession, supplication and intercession. It is the presence of the Holy Spirit in the group that gives direction to the prayer life of the group.

We will speak elsewhere about the prayer life of the church but we cannot pass without emphasizing that every group needs to be a praying group: a group that longs for the presence of God, both personally and corporately. Jesus demonstrated the importance of prayer to his own disciples. It was an indispensable part of their training, which in turn they would pass on to others. One thing is certain: unless they grasped the meaning of prayer and learnt how to practice it with consistency, they could never demonstrate the power which they knew was available.

It is often in this context of waiting upon God in prayer in a small group that the gifts of the Holy Spirit become manifest.

Our leaders are offered a separate training course in all aspects of leading a group, not least the use of spiritual gifts. Discovering, developing and using spiritual gifts must be one of the continuums of church, just like Bible study, prayer and the breaking of bread.

Chapter 6, 'Dead Men Don't Eat Lunch', deals with the diet of a healthy church so you may be surprised that I did not mention there the prime importance of the Bible study. I am hoping you take that as a given, but it needs to be more than just a Bible study. It needs to be a devotional Bible study because the Christian life depends on the devotional. Systematic Bible study is necessary but this can be pursued in the larger meetings of the church. In devotional Bible studies the aim is not so much to instruct the mind as to inflame the heart. A passage of scripture can be selected and either commented on by the leader or discussed amongst the group. The whole object is to feed on Christ through his Word. It is important that the passage be understood in its context, but one must go beyond that to discover its up-to-date message. That message must then be allowed to speak to the heart, the mind and the conscience.

It is important to ring the changes in the methods used in our approach. A wise leader will sometimes invite members of the group to introduce the Bible study. There will always be questions asked to stimulate conversation. Time will be provided for further questions to be asked. Here again, the devotional aspect should not be missed. Everything should be done in a relaxed manner, avoiding a 'classroom' atmosphere at all costs.

Again, the facilitating of a devotional Bible study shared by a group is another matter covered in the Leadership Training Course.

Last but not least is the habit of eating together, if circumstances permit. This is a wonderful way of creating an atmosphere of community. All these aspects of our life together – sharing, caring, praying, studying, eating together – are part of *koinonia*. Such a fellowship helps Christians to develop in their lived discipleship.

Members of the group will want to come along and they will want to invite others. What is more, when others know the good time being enjoyed by all, they will want to come. Healthy cells multiply, a fact which may present a problem and challenge, but wise leaders know how to handle this. New groups are born and the Body of Jesus Christ is found to be growing in a healthy way.

The church that seemed in slumber
has now risen from its knees
And dry bones are responding
with the fruits of new birth...[25]

Chapter 9

'I Only Want to Glorify the King'

Ronnie Wilson's hymn 'I Hear the Sound of Rustling in the
Leaves of the Trees' ended the last chapter and with the chorus
from that hymn we continue our theme of dry bones responding
with the fruits of new birth:

I only want to be his breath,
I only want to glorify the King.

Christian worship, at its best, is an experience of heaven on earth.
Tragically, at its worst, so-called worship services can for some
seem more like hell. Such are the highs and lows of our
experience. I have known both and it has little to do with
numbers, buildings, musicians, choirs or liturgy. It has everything to do with the manifest presence of God among the
worshiping community.

Let me share with you two contrasting stories.

In February 1996 I was ministering in Sri Lanka. One
particular meeting was held in Aglawatta, south east of the
capital city, Colombo. The very spartan building was built out of
breezeblocks with corrugated iron for a roof. There were no
windows or doors. There were no musicians, only a gathering of
about 20 adults and a number of children. After what seemed a
quiet service at which I spoke, the church leader, Pastor Nimal,
called everyone to prayer. They rose as one, including the
children, hands raised and faces looking towards heaven, and all
started praying audibly at the same time. What a sound! I had a
very clear picture of them laying down a bridge between earth
and heaven across which God in his sovereignty was coming

amongst us. There was an awesome sense of the presence of God. A silence fell and there was a prophetic word that simply said that God's power was among us to heal. I have never been in a worship service quite like it. They were agonizing for more of God.

Later the same evening, in Sri Lanka's Tamil hill country, in a small, crowded rubber-plantation cottage where a recently planted church held its meetings, the presence of God began to manifest his power. At first there was a simple children's story mainly for the benefit of the 20 youngsters, at the end of which 12 people made a commitment to Christ.

Pastor Nimal Ranjith Costa rose again and said, 'We are going to continue to worship God and then Pastor John is going to preach properly!' When I had finished, the pastor asked me to sit down. Arranging a chair alongside me for the sick to be brought to, he reminded everyone of God's presence to heal. One by one, people came forward with the expectation that God was going to heal them.

The first to come was a father, a deacon of the church at Aglawatta, with his little daughter who hopped towards me. The interpreter told me she had palsy; her little hand was deformed but as we prayed in Jesus' name her hand took on normal shape and form. I found it almost unbelievable; the people just shouted, 'It's a miracle!'

Her father said, 'But what about her leg?' So I told the girl to walk, in Jesus' name, and she did! He ran outside shouting, 'It's a miracle!' And there was a rush into that cottage such as I have never seen! It was a Hindu community and the villagers were queuing up to come and experience the presence of God. Christians were leaving the cottage to make room for others to come in. For four hours people kept coming and falling down under the sense of the presence of God. That night, a Hindu community became a Christian community.

Since that time, 14 new churches have been planted and

growth continues in that small region of Sri Lanka. That service had all the hallmarks of authentic revival. What made it so remarkable was the awesome sense of the presence of God amongst an ordinary group of people who lacked any theological training, facilities and the technology that seems so important to us in the West.

A year earlier, in 1995, I was traveling in the United States of America, having opportunities to speak at a number of large churches. I had the privilege of attending a church with a congregation of 15,000 people in attendance. The building was a Baptist cathedral, one of the finest in the USA, with a car park that covered many acres. There were more staff than most churches in the United Kingdom have members. The choir, suitably robed and with a professional sound, was the backdrop to a beautifully orchestrated act of public worship. As I looked out onto the congregation, I had never seen a sight like it; it looked like an audience of wooden dolls. I do not doubt that those on the platform were worshiping but this large congregation was not engaged; to me, the greatest tragedy of all was that I didn't sense anything of the presence of God.

Now these two stories from my experience may be a million miles away from the 'normal' life of the majority of Christians. So why do I tell the stories? To illustrate that worship services, to be effective and inspiring, have nothing to do with buildings, music, numbers nor a host of other things that we consider to be indispensable. Rather the key is experiencing worship in spirit and in reality.

John's Gospel records the story for us of a Samaritan woman whom Jesus met at a well. The Lord Jesus came to challenge her about her life and lifestyle. When she felt he was getting a bit too close to the bone, she asked him a 'religious' question.

'Sir,' the woman said, 'I can see that you are a prophet. Our fathers worshiped on this mountain, but you Jews claim that the place where we must worship is in Jerusalem.'

Jesus declared, 'Believe me, woman, a time is coming when you will worship the Father neither on this mountain nor in Jerusalem. You Samaritans worship what you do not know; we worship what we do know, for salvation is from the Jews. Yet a time is coming and has now come when the two worshipers will worship the Father in spirit and truth, for they are the kind of worshipers the Father seeks. God is spirit, and his worshipers must worship in spirit and in truth.

John 4:19–24

The Lord Jesus went straight to the heart of the matter, making a contrast between false and true worship.

False worship is based not on the revelation of God but on the imagination of men and women. We are often told by people today that they worship God in their own way.

Worship in Spirit and Reality

Jesus spelt out the heart of true worship. He said it must be in spirit. As such, it is not limited to things or places. Of course it is lovely to have a nice building to worship in, gifted musicians and singers, trained and articulate ministers to lead worship. But having all of that does not guarantee that we will know the necessary sense of the Spirit of God. If God is Spirit, we can only engage with him as we worship under the anointing which the Holy Spirit gives. The only gifts that are acceptable to God in worship are the manifestations of the Spirit – love, loyalty, obedience and devotion.

True worship does not consist of coming to a certain place nor in going through a certain ritual or liturgy nor even in bringing certain gifts. Real worship is when our human spirit speaks to, hears from and engages with God.

Not only must worship be in spirit but in truth – that is, reality. Worship relates to the whole life of worshipers, not just to the religious part. William Temple, a former Archbishop of Canterbury, perhaps gave the best definition of worship:

> Worship is the submission of all of our nature to God. It is the quickening of the conscience by his holiness; the nourishment of mind with his truth; the purifying of imagination by his beauty; the opening of the heart to his love; the surrender of will to his purpose – and all this is gathered up in adoration, the most selfless emotion of which our nature is capable.[26]

Such worship, encompassing the whole of life, should be reflected in our worship services which will seek to engage not only with God but with the world, life and the whole person, moving mind, heart and hands. It will inspire and affect people with various emotions. It will be successful in helping them to apply their faith to the ordinary world. The role of the priest has always been to represent the world to God, and God to the world. That must be the function of the church in worship today. Healthy churches will therefore be churches that seek to worship God in spirit and in truth.

Are there biblical patterns that can help us examine worship? Let us seek an illustration from both the Old Testament and the New Testament.

An Old Testament Illustration

We are not given a great deal of specific information in the Bible regarding the form which was adopted when the Old Testament saints came together to worship. The book of Leviticus was written as a manual for the priests to follow. It provides an outline of how people can approach a Holy God.

Leviticus and Exodus 25 – 31 provide instructions about the building of the tabernacle. God spoke to Moses in the 'Tent of Meeting', the tabernacle. It was God's home amongst his people and the place where he both met them collectively in worship and also revealed himself to significant individuals, such as Moses and Aaron, to make his will known. It was placed in the center of the camp, with the tribes around it, as a visual reminder that the worship of God needed to be central to every aspect of their life. The design of the tabernacle was by divine revelation. It spoke of how people were to approach God.

Solomon's temple in Jerusalem was built on the same design. The synagogue service was developed later and was created due to the fact that the temple was destroyed and God's people were exiled in Babylon. It seemed to include the following:

- The *Shema* or Jewish Creed
- Psalms and music
- Sacrifice and offerings
- Prayers
- Readings from the scriptures
- Exposition

Following the exile to Babylon, God appointed leaders who would be responsible for the return to the land, and the rebuilding of both the temple and the areas of Jerusalem where the people would live. They were also charged with the restoration of the public reading of scripture and the corporate worship of the people of God. All of this was with a view to re-establishing the covenant relationship between God and his people through unity of vision and purpose.

After the temple and the city had been rebuilt, we have a beautiful illustration of God's people at worship. It is recorded for us in Nehemiah chapters 8 to 9. There are at least three important principles that should be underlined from this Old Testament illustration of worship.

The centrality of the Word of God
First, we cannot help but notice the important place the scrip-

tures held. 'They told Ezra the scribe to bring out the Book of the Law of Moses' (Nehemiah 8:1). The people were hungry for the Word of God.

> Ezra opened the book. All the people could see him because he was standing above them and as he opened it the people all stood up. Ezra praised the Lord, the great God; and all the people lifted up their hands and responded, 'Amen! Amen!' Then they bowed down with their faces to the ground.
> Nehemiah 8:5

We can sense the anticipation and expectation. However, it was not just a matter of reading the Word; there was understanding and application of it as seen here: 'They read from the Book of the Law of God, making it clear and giving the meaning so that the people could understand what was being read' (Nehemiah 8:8).

• They read the text of God's Word: 'They read from the Book of the Law of God, making it clear'. The King James Version says that 'they read God's Word distinctly'. The practice of reading the scriptures should constitute a regular discipline in the quiet time we have with God. But more than this, when we come together, we need to ensure that the public reading of scripture is done well and with clarity.

• They revealed the truth of God's Word: 'and giving the meaning'. The people understand what was being said. It has been well said that a text out of context is a pretext. Preachers need to remember this, also recalling with St Augustine that 'when the scriptures speak, God speaks'.

• They related the thrust of God's Word: 'the people could understand what was being read'. This refers to the application of the Word of God. After hearing some people preach, I find myself asking the question, 'So what?' We all need to ask the question, 'What was the effect of this exposition of the Word of God?' Ezra ensured that this was no mere academic approach. He and his hearers wanted their lives and their worship to match the Word of God.

The effect of the public reading of scripture is seen in verse 14: 'They found written in the Law, which the Lord had commanded through Moses, that the Israelites were to live in booths during the feast of the seventh month.' They were in Jerusalem celebrating the Feast of Tabernacles (also called the Feast of the Seventh Month and the Festival of Booths). During this feast the Jews were supposed to live in temporary shelters as a reminder that when the Lord delivered them from slavery in Egypt they had to rely totally on him. However, this practice had not been reinstated after the exile. The discovery of it here in the scriptures was a challenge to them. A proclamation was made: 'Go out into the hill country and bring back branches from olive and wild olive trees, and from myrtles, palms and shade trees, to make booths – as it is written' (verse 15). The people responded immediately.

We must always be bringing our lives and what we do as the church under the judgment of scripture. We should judge scripture less and allow scripture to judge us and our practices more. We cannot vault over a certain passage in the Bible because we do not like it, because it hurts us, or because it does not fit in with our preconceived ideas.

Dr Raymond Brown, formerly Principal of Spurgeon's College, London, is the author of *The Message of Nehemiah*. He writes,

The relevant application of Scripture is of paramount importance.

It is not a book which simply describes life in the world of antiquity; it is a message for today; vibrant with meaningful up to date application...perhaps the *application* of Scripture is the hardest aspect of both personal Bible study and Christian preaching but, in both cases, personal reader and public preacher must struggle hard to bridge the gap between what we have read and what we must do.[27]

The reality of the worship Of God

The second thing we observe from this Old Testament illustration is how real their expression of worship was: 'Ezra praised the Lord, the great God; and all the people lifted their hands and responded, 'Amen! Amen!' Then they bowed down and worshiped the Lord with their faces to the ground.' There are two observations that we should make.

• Their worship was spontaneous without being unthinking. They realized that something holy was happening, something wonderful was taking place, and they responded spontaneously. There is no trace of the leaders whipping up emotions. The people were responding spontaneously to the Holy Spirit's presence.

• Their worship was demonstrative without being theatrical. This lifting up of hands, spontaneous cries of 'Amen', and bowing down and worshiping the Lord with their faces to the ground was not a show – they could not help themselves. They wanted to demonstrate their love and their thanks to God and so should we.

A child stretching up its arms to a loving parent does not have to say a word; the parent knows exactly what it wants. When we come to worship, we come to a loving heavenly Father to express how we feel about him and to demonstrate our desire to be closer to him.

Observe that 'all' of the people lifted their hands, 'all' responded 'Amen! Amen!', 'all' bowed down and worshiped the Lord with their faces to the ground. This was no audience but rather a congregation united in this purpose.

The sincerity of the people's response to God

We have already observed the response at the beginning of the feast. The people saw the need to correct the way in which they were celebrating that Jewish festival and they brought their ways into line with the Word of God. However, there is an even greater response observed at the end of the celebration: 'In view of all this we are making a binding agreement, putting it in writing, and our leaders, our Levites and our priests are affixing their seals to it' (Nehemiah 9:38). In chapter 9 we read of another occasion when the people gathered for a time of public confession, when they fasted and wore sackcloth (9:1). Nehemiah led the prayer of confession. Confession is still considered an important part of public worship. There is in this chapter a wonderful contrast expressed so beautifully in their prayer, a contrast between the faithfulness of God and the infidelity of his people. Having confessed their sins, they express their desire to re-establish the covenant with God (9:38).

Every time we come to worship as a congregation, we need to make the same contrasts between God's faithfulness and our infidelity. What amazing grace God shows us! How faithful he is in keeping his promises and longing to forgive us, despite the failure, foolishness and weakness displayed in our lives!

This is an account of the renewal of the Old Covenant; what, we might ask, should it say about our celebration of the New Covenant at the Lord's Supper? When the Apostle Paul wrote to the Corinthian church about their worship services, he had to deal with some abuses of worship. One of his concerns was the way in which they celebrated 'the breaking of bread' (1 Corinthians 11:17–34).

The careless and unthinking celebrations of the Corinthian Christians violated the very idea of covenant. Paul reminded them that through the shedding of the blood of Jesus, the paschal lamb, it was now possible for every believer to know the joy of sins forgiven and enter into a personal relationship with God. But those who enter into a covenant relationship with the Lord naturally enter at the same time into a covenant relationship with one another. If the love of Christ is not evident in our relationships with other believers, then, whatever we do at the communion table, it is not 'The Lord's Supper'.

The Lord's Supper should be a time when we reflect on our relationship with the Lord and with one another and reaffirm our covenant both vertically and horizontally.

A New Testament Illustration

As we examine the New Testament, we discover the same principles are present: the centrality of the Word of God, the reality of the worship of God and the sincerity of the response to God. The Day of Pentecost, when the church was born, shows the same characteristics.

We have just been considering Paul's first letter to the Corinthians and there is a most interesting and instructive passage a little further on: 'What then shall we say, brothers? When you come together, everyone has a hymn, or a word of instruction, a revelation, a tongue or an interpretation. All of these must be done for the strengthening of the church' (1 Corinthians 14:26). Clearly, 'coming together' for public worship was a common experience. Paul envisages a congregation rather than an audience. Every member of the church is expected to bring a distinctive contribution to the worship. Again the emphasis is clear: the meeting is not for the purpose of entertainment but rather for edification, that is, for the 'strengthening' of the church. Two needs are stressed in this verse.

1. The need for authority. Whilst the worship was open to anyone who had a gift to use it, what follows in the rest of this chapter is a plan for orderly worship. Corinth was obviously blessed with many gifted members. Paul reminds them that the true test of spirituality is not arrogance and self-assertion but rather submission to the authority of those set over them in the Lord. So he reminds those prophets in the congregation that they must be 'subject to the control of prophets' (14:32). Paul also emphasizes the call to recognize the authority behind his

remarks: 'If anybody thinks he is a prophet or spiritually gifted, let him acknowledge that what I am writing to you is the Lord's command' (14:37). Any tendency to think we are right while the rest of the church is wrong is both arrogant and dangerous.

Thank God that he led the early church fathers to collect the books and letters which we now have as the New Testament, placing them in the canon of scripture alongside the Old Testament. Every other 'revelation' made in a worship service must be tested against the truth of God's Word.

2. The need for flexibility. In the Corinthian congregation, things were obviously informal enough to allow everyone who felt inspired by the Spirit to share a message, to give it. This clearly works best in a relatively small group of people. Remember that Paul is probably thinking of the different home churches, such as that held in the home of Aquila and Priscilla. Nevertheless the principle of flexibility must still apply even when there are thousands in the congregation. Prepare for worship we must, but not so much that there is no room for the Holy Spirit to move.

Spirit-filled worshipers want to be participants, not spectators. People will come prepared to share what God has given, not a result of intellectual ability but because of spiritual awareness and intimacy. With the growth of a new awareness of spiritual gifts as well as anointed natural gifts, even the most unlikely individuals, emotionally and temperamentally, are prepared to make an offering to the building up of the Body of Christ. The principle is clear: as many as meaningfully and spiritually can take part should do so.

Frustrations in Worship

After 40 years of leading congregations in worship, I find it more difficult than ever. Having traveled widely and worshiped in just about every sort of congregation, I must confess that all too often I find services dissatisfying, disappointing and very frustrating.

I realize that the experience in Aglawatta, Sri Lanka, is rare and can only be attributed to the sovereign purposes of God. Yet worship ought not to be the source of such dissatisfaction that it is.

Tabernacle, Penarth has not been immune from the pain of transitioning from a traditional form of worship to one that aims to be convergent of the best. However, in 1991 we adopted amongst others this goal relating to worship: 'To ensure that the worship on Sunday is God-pleasing, scripturally honoring and personally edifying'.

As a step towards achieving the goal, a working party was appointed to review and consider all aspects of worship, and the church was asked to support the working party with prayer and a readiness to bring into practice their proposals. They produced an excellent report that has been foundational to our future development and transition. Amongst their conclusions was this:

> The conclusion must be that there is no one 'right' form of worship for all times and all places. On the contrary, worship is dynamic and while its objective – to glorify God – always remains the same, the way in which people worship shows many variations. Worship should be regarded as being more like the ever-changing movement of the sea rather than the absolute stillness of the millpond.

Principles to Provide Guidance

There is always a tension in a loving relationship but principles were established to provide guidance not only to the planners and leaders of worship but also the whole congregation. Those four principles were:

1. Worship should be pleasing to God.
2. The contents and other elements should conform to scripture.

3. Worship should be corporate in nature.
4. Worship should have regard to the needs of the entire congregation and be relevant to them.

Pleasing to God

It should always be the motivation of discipleship to please God. After all, it was the Lord Jesus who said that he lived to please his Father. This is particularly important in regard to worship: the primary object should be to please God, not the congregation. The scriptures make it clear that worship can only be pleasing to God when the worshipers are leading lives which are pleasing to him. There is no true worship which does not result in a life of obedience.

This is what the Lord says:

I hate, I despise your religious feasts;
I cannot stand your assemblies.
Even though you bring me burnt offerings and grain offerings,
I will not accept them.
Though you bring choice fellowship offerings,
I will have no regard for them.
Away with the noise of your songs!
I will not listen to the music of your harps.
But let justice roll on like a river,
righteousness like a never-failing stream!
Amos 5:21–24

Of course God loves worship, music and singing. These are all of his design, but such acts of worship make him sick if they are expressions of an empty religion. True worship must make a difference to the way we live our lives. The Lord was displeased with the Jews' worship on the Sabbath and at the Festivals because it was not reflected in their lives as the people of God.

The writer to the Hebrews is divinely inspired and sums it up beautifully: 'Through Jesus, therefore, let us continually offer to God a sacrifice of praise – the fruit of lips that confess his name. And do not forget to do good and to share with others, for with such sacrifices God is pleased' (Hebrews 13:15–16). Christian worship must be a '24/7' activity; what happens in the sanctuary should be a reflection of our lives in the home, workplace and world. When it isn't, the Lord knows – and it makes him sick!

If we are to please God in our worship then we must be right with God and with one another. But more than that, worship should be the best of which we are capable, and everything should be done decently and in order. Quality, particularly when it comes to music, is subjective, but that does not relieve the church of the responsibility to exercise its judgment concerning what should and should not be used.

Conformity with scripture

We have already established that Holy Scripture is our God-given authority and should guide us in what elements (for example, prayer, preaching, singing, artistic expression) we include in our worship and also the content (that is. the theology) of our worship. This is not to suggest that we should exclude from worship anything not specifically mentioned in the scriptures, but rather that we need to test all elements and practices which might be included in our worship to ensure they conform to the teaching of scripture. We are concerned that the theology of our hymns, prayers and preaching should conform to scripture; any material which does not meet this test should be excluded.

Corporate nature

Worship can be an individual activity as well as a corporate activity. But when the church meets together to worship as a congregation, it is essential that the corporate nature of worship should be acknowledged. Because it is corporate it is unlikely that everything done will please the entire congregation all of the time. Some of it may even displease individuals, but if the worship is pleasing to God then it is important that individuals should not feel aggrieved or be critical of others in the congregation but that we should continue to obey the commandment of Christ to 'love each other' (John 15:12).

God clearly delights in diversity and one way that diversity is expressed is in the difference between individuals. He also expects us to worship corporately, and corporate activity of any kind always involves some degree of subordination of the individual. In this case it involves the subordination of some of our individual likes and dislikes in worship.

Relevance to congregational needs
While our worship should be pleasing to God above all and should be directed to that end, it is clearly important that the content and structure of worship should also be relevant to as many of the worshipers as possible. Because of our diversity, individual needs and tastes will vary. It is not reasonable to expect that all of those variations can be fully catered for in every service. It is, however, essential that every service should be designed with the intention of sending worshipers away satisfied.

Always remember that we are at a worship service first and foremost for the Lord.

When the music fades
and all is stripped away…
it's all about you, Jesus.[28]

Motivation for Worship
The English word 'worship' derives from the Saxon *werothscipe* which became 'worthship' or the acknowledgement of worth.

Therefore to worship God means to acknowledge God's worth, to give him the glory. Christian worship must always be Trinitarian. We give the Father glory by honoring his Son the Lord Jesus Christ in the power which the Holy Spirit provides.

The revelation of heaven's worship provides both the best illustration of worship and a clear outline of motivations for worship:

Whenever the living creatures give glory, honor and thanks to him who sits on the throne and who lives for ever and ever, the twenty-four elders fall down before him who sits on the throne, and worship him who lives for ever and ever. They lay their crowns before the throne and say:

'You are worthy, our Lord and God,
to receive glory and honor and power,
for you created all things,
and by your will they were created
and have their being.'

Then I saw in the right hand of him who sat on the throne a scroll with writing on both sides and sealed with seven seals. And I saw a mighty angel proclaiming in a loud voice, 'Who is worthy to break the seals and open the scroll?' But no-one in heaven or on earth or under the earth could open the scroll or even look inside it. I wept and wept because no-one was found who was worthy to open the scroll or look inside. Then one of the elders said to me, 'Do not weep! See, the Lion of the tribe of Judah, the Root of David, has triumphed. He is able to open the scroll and its seven seals.'

Then I saw a Lamb, looking as if it had been slain, standing in the centre of the throne, encircled by the four living creatures and the elders. He had seven horns and seven eyes, which are the seven spirits of God sent out into all the earth.

He came and took the scroll from the right hand of him who sat on the throne. And when he had taken it, the four living creatures and the twenty-four elders fell down before the Lamb. Each one had a harp and they were holding golden bowls full of incense, which are the prayers of the saints. And they sang a new song:

'You are worthy to take the scroll

and to open its seals,

because you were slain,

and with your blood you purchased men for God

from every tribe and language and people and nation.

You have made them to be a kingdom and priests to serve our God,

and they will reign on the earth.'

Then I looked and heard the voice of many angels, numbering thousands upon thousands, and ten thousand times ten thousand. They encircled the throne and the living creatures and the elders. In a loud voice they sang:

'Worthy is the Lamb, who was slain,

to receive power and wealth and wisdom and strength

and honor and glory and praise!'

Then I heard every creature in heaven and on earth and under the earth and on the sea, and all that is in them, singing:

'To him who sits on the throne and to the Lamb

be praise and honor and glory and power,

for ever and ever!'

The four living creatures said, 'Amen', and the elders fell down and worshiped.

Revelation 4:9 – 5:4

The Father is seeking such worshipers: those who will worship him in Spirit and in truth. We cannot worship in the Spirit alone, for the Spirit without truth is helpless. We cannot worship in truth alone, for that would be a theology without life. Worship must be in Spirit and in truth.

The tragedy is that much that is called 'worship' today is unacceptable to God. Without the inspiration of the Holy Spirit, there can be no true worship. We must humbly worship God in Spirit and in truth.

Chapter 10

Prayer: The Church's Lifeline

Claude is a hunter. He is our family cat, ginger in color and looking like a lion. His natural instinct is to catch anything that moves in the garden. Children are quite safe but birds and any form of rodent had better watch out. Not that he is hungry, for his method is merely strategic: he just goes for the neck of bird or mouse, chokes the life out of them and then brings them to the garden patio as a trophy of his hunting prowess. Being lovers of creation, we do not approve of his actions but they serve as a valuable illustration.

'Be self-controlled and alert. Your enemy the devil prowls around like a roaring lion looking for someone to devour' (1 Peter 5:8). Our archenemy's strategy is the same as Claude's: to go for the lifeline. If he can stop us praying, he has scored a major victory.

> Prayer is the Christian's vital breath,
> The Christian's native air,
> His watchword at the gates of death;
> He enters heaven with prayer.[29]

Healthy churches have overcome every obstacle and learnt the power of corporate prayer. Study the stories of every church that has grown significantly and you will see that prayer is given a high priority in the church's program – not necessarily in the form of a traditional weekly prayer meeting but rather they have found creative ways for their own particular church to persevere in prayer together.

Again we ask the question: What did Jesus say? At the

beginning and towards the end of his ministry it is recorded:

> Jesus entered the temple area and drove out all who were buying and selling there. He overturned the tables of the moneychangers and the benches of those selling doves. 'It is written,' he said to them, "My house will be called a house of prayer," but you are making it a "den of robbers".'
> Matthew 21:12–13

Our Lord is quoting Isaiah's prophecy that predicts the coming of the King, the Messiah, to right the wrong in the nation. All of the programs and purposes of the local church need to come under the scrutiny of King Jesus. We need to ask ourselves what has become superfluous to Kingdom purposes and whether we need to correct matters. A devotion to corporate prayer is an obvious answer.

The church of Jerusalem knew what they were called to: 'They devoted themselves to the apostles' teaching and to the fellowship, to the breaking of bread and to prayer' (Acts 2:42). It is significant that their devotion to public praying is mentioned last. Praying together is the natural development of a devotion to the Word of God, church fellowship and the breaking of bread. If the first three aspects of Christian faith and practice are not vital factors in our personal and corporate life then praying together is nothing more than a farce.

The Lord Jesus made it quite clear in his teaching that failure to be devoted to praying was a sign of spiritual weakness. 'Jesus told his disciples a parable to show them that they should always pray and not give up' (Luke 18:1).

There is a wonderful illustration of that Jerusalem church at prayer recorded for us in Acts 4:

> As soon as Peter and John were let go [from prison], they went to their friends and told them what the high priests and

religious leaders had said. Hearing the report, they lifted their voices in a wonderful harmony in prayer: 'Strong God, you made heaven and earth and sea and everything in them. By the Holy Spirit you spoke through the mouth of your servant and our father, David:

"Why the big noise, nations?

Why the mean plots, peoples?

Earth's leaders push for position,

Potentates meet for summit talks,

The God-deniers, the Messiah-defiers!"

For in fact they did meet – Herod and Pontius Pilate with nations and peoples, even Israel itself! – met in this very city to plot against your holy Son Jesus, the one you made Messiah, to carry out the plans you long ago set in motion.

And now they're at it again! Take care of their threats and give your servants fearless confidence in preaching your message, as you stretch out your hand to us in healings and miracles and wonders done in the name of your holy servant Jesus.'

While they were praying, the place where they were meeting trembled and shook. They were all filled with the Holy Spirit and continued to speak God's Word with fearless confidence.

Acts 4:23–31 *The Message*

Peter and John had been imprisoned; immediately upon their release they joined the Christian congregation in Jerusalem and reported all that had been happening to them. They had been beaten and warned never to preach in the name of Jesus again. When the Christians heard their report what did they do? Did they declare a moratorium on future meetings? Did they set up a working party to review and report on the problems? No, they simply prayed instinctively and immediately. Prayer was funda- mental and they all felt the same about it.

There is only one real problem in the church of the twenty-first century and that problem is the prayer life of the church. Of course, there are many other problems but this is the *real* problem. When a church solves that problem, it has found the way to resolving other issues. All of our difficulties would more easily be settled if the prayer life of the local church became vital and powerful.

When we analyze Peter's prayer a number of lessons emerge for us to imitate as we seek to create praying churches.

Focus on the Lord

The early believers were not focusing on the problem of persecution or the limitations that had been imposed upon them. They focused on God.

• 'Sovereign Lord...you made the heaven and the earth and the sea and everything in them... They did what your power and will had decided beforehand should happen' (Acts 4:24, 28). It is evident that they believed in an all-powerful Creator who was providentially at work through the experiences and setbacks of life.

• 'You spoke by the Holy Spirit through the mouth of your servant our father, David' (verse 25). Their focus was on the Word of God: what he had said through the prophets but most clearly in God's Son.

Where are our prayers focused? On the problems or on the one Person who can change the circumstances or give us the grace to overcome them? Whatever problems face us, it is God who matters, not the meeting, nor the man nor money – these are always secondary. Our focus on the Sovereign Lord makes our prayers count.

Pray with a Purpose

The Jerusalem church knew their purpose and calling. It was to be witnesses to Christ. So they prayed, 'Now, Lord, consider their threats and enable your servants to speak your word with great boldness' (Acts 4:29).

It would have been so easy for them to pray for safety and protection. They might have prayed that there would be no recurrence of the problems they were experiencing. But that was not their purpose in praying. Their purpose was to ask God for the boldness to make known the Good News. In a praying church the overwhelming desire of the members will be to make Jesus Christ known to a lost world. This will be clear when you listen to the prayers.

Have Faith to Request Miracles
'Stretch out your hand to heal and perform miraculous signs and wonders through the name of your holy servant Jesus' (Acts 4:30). The church in Jerusalem prayed for signs and wonders. When the church really prays, miracles take place. Souls are saved, disciples are made, and God is often pleased to heal the minds and bodies of those who are sick.

The miracles witnessed in the church at Aglawatta, referred to in the last chapter, are not commonplace in churches in the United Kingdom. However, we have seen verifiable miracles: the blind receiving their sight, arthritis sufferers healed, a curvature of the spine straightened, a sufferer of tinnitus healed. I could go on to make a very impressive list that would span a period of 40 years. However, even though such miracles are rare in the 'developed' nations at this time, answers to prayer are not. The prayers of righteous people are still powerful and effective.

We praise God for miracles within the fellowship and worship or in people's homes as we anoint them with oil and lay hands on them, but we also pray for doctors, nurses, therapists, hospital workers and those involved in medical research, through whom God also works miracles on a daily basis. These are some of the 'greater things' the Lord Jesus promised; more miracles occur today through modern medicine than ever happened in the days of Jesus' flesh.

See Manifestations of the Presence and Power of God
'After they prayed, the place where they were meeting was shaken. And they were all filled with the Holy Spirit and spoke the word of God boldly' (Acts 4:31).

Prayer is the secret of every renewal and revival. Before the Holy Spirit came at Pentecost, the church had been locked together in prayer for ten days. In the history of revivals there is a clear pattern. There are periods of intense corporate prayer preceding the visitations of God. The only hope for the world today is a mighty outpouring of the Holy Spirit on the church.

A praying church is a congregation of believers who pray not only individually but together. If the Acts of the Apostles provides an illustration of a praying church, we must look to the epistles to provide the characteristics of our prayer life together. For this we turn to Paul's magnificent treatment of the subject in Timothy 2:1–8. The Apostle Paul intends that corporate praying should be intelligent and all-embracing so he outlines the distinctive features that should characterize any gathering for praise, prayer and worship. 'I urge, then, first of all, that requests, prayers, intercession and thanksgiving be made for everyone – for kings and all those in authority, that we may live peaceful and quiet lives in all godliness and holiness' (1 Timothy 2:1–2).

The Characteristics of Corporate Prayer
Four elements are to be present:

• 'Requests' (2:1). In the King James Version this word is translated 'supplications'. This is praying on the basis of the mercy of God. A father may request of God the recovery of his sick child, but the answer is entirely with Almighty God as to whether it is better to take or heal the child. Our requests are always on the basis of the grace and the mercy of God.

• 'Prayers' (2:1). Prayer is an act of worship not just an

expression of wants and needs. There should be reverence in our hearts as we pray to God. However, prayers are prayed in confidence because they are prayed on the basis of the promises of God. To pray in this way we need to know the Bible and so be aware of the promises in God's Word. Praying like this is simply 'standing on the promises of God'.

• 'Intercession' (2:1). This is praying on the basis of the promises of God. The word might also be translated 'petitions'. In 1 Timothy 4:5 the same word is used to refer to blessing the food we eat. The core meaning is to come close to a person and communicate intimately with him or her. It suggests that we intercede on the basis of our fellowship with God.

• 'Thanksgiving' (2:1). This is praying on the basis of the goodness of God. We give thanks not only for answers to prayer but for who God is and for what he does for us in his grace. We should not simply add our thanksgiving to the end of a selfish prayer.

I can remember more than a few occasions when no other form of prayer seemed to be prevailing and I have heard the whisper, 'Try thanksgiving.' The biblical warrant is plain: 'Give thanks in all circumstances, for this is God's will for you in Christ Jesus' (1 Thessalonians 5:16). Thanksgiving works at restoring peace and removing anxiety. No one has truly prayed unless they can say, 'Thank you, Lord!'

The Comprehensiveness of Corporate Prayer
'I urge...prayers...be made for everyone - for kings and all those in authority, that we may live peaceful and quiet lives in all godliness and holiness' (1 Timothy 2:1–2). This means that all kinds and conditions of people are to be prayed for. The task is not a simple or an easy one, but is clearly our Christian responsibility. This is all the more remarkable when you realize that Emperor Nero was on the throne at the time this was written and yet the believers were supposed to pray for him. There is the

need to make a distinction between the person and the position.

In the second century, Polycarp of Smyrna bears testimony to this practice in the church. He says, 'Pray for all the saints, pray, too, for all kings and powers and rulers, and for your persecutors, and those that hate you, and for your cruel enemies.' These words sum up what Paul means by 'everyone'. If they are to be the objects of our praying together then there is no doubt what the outcome should be. We are to pray that 'we may live peaceful and quiet lives in all godliness and holiness. This is good, and pleases God our Savior' (2 Timothy 2:2–3). Prayer of itself is a good practice but it brings many benefits. However, such prayer is also pleasing to the Lord. If our prayers are to please God then clearly they must be in line with the will of God. It certainly does not please the Father when we pray selfishly.

What pleases the Father is when our prayers comprehensively include our communities, nations and world. God acts in response to prayer for peace and reconciliation through the political leaders we are urged to pray for. My understanding of the importance of praying for peace and reconciliation has been greatly helped by visits to Northern Ireland. Two organizations, known to me, have been active both prayerfully and practically in making a significant difference.

The Centre for Contemporary Christianity in Ireland is committed to helping Christians serve Christ and our changing world, effectively. Formerly known as ECONI (Evangelical Contribution on Northern Ireland), this group has produced a plethora of books and publications that have informed our thinking and praying since it was formed in 1987. I commend its quarterly newsletter, 'Lion and Lamb', as a most useful resource. The members work and pray in a political and spiritual minefield but they have played a key role in establishing the peace that is currently being enjoyed.

The other organization is the community at the Christian Renewal Centre in Rostrevor which was founded in 1974 as a group of Christians drawn together by God from different churches, both Catholic and Protestant, and since then also from other newer expressions of church. They seek, through the power of the Holy Spirit, to demonstrate and proclaim the uniting love of Jesus Christ. God called them to pray and work for reconciliation, through prayer and renewal, in his church in Ireland and abroad. Having visited them on a number of occasions, I bear witness to the difference that they have made in community relationships. It is still true: 'The prayer of a righteous man is powerful and effective' (James 5.18).

Another outcome of such praying will be the salvation of men and women. 'This is good, and pleases God our Savior, who wants all men to be saved and come to the knowledge of the truth' (1 Timothy 2:3–4). God has ordained that through praying he will add to the Kingdom such as should be saved. It has been a tremendous encouragement to me over the years to remember that 'he is patient with you, not wanting anyone to perish, but everyone to come to repentance' (2 Peter 3:9).

The Conditions of Corporate Prayer

'I want men everywhere to lift up holy hands in prayer, without anger or disputing' (1 Timothy 2:8). Whether in private or corporate prayer, there are certain conditions which determine whether our prayers will be effective. Paul makes it clear what these conditions are here.

We are to pray 'lifting up holy hands'. It was the Jewish practice to lift up the hands not only when taking a solemn oath or blessing others but also when praying. In such an attitude of prayer, however, the hands were to be holy, that is, unstained with deliberate sin.

Another condition is that we must pray 'without anger or disputing'. Bitterness towards God or an unforgiving spirit towards another believer undermines prayer. The psalmist reminds us that if we regard iniquity in our hearts then the Lord will not hear us (Psalm 66:18 KJV).

A healthy church will be a church that explores ways in which it can pray and gives thanks for every indication of God in the community, nation and world. It will then create opportunities for believers to pray together and have regard for what constitutes a praying church and the prayers it offers.

Chapter 11

'Like a Mighty Army!'

Joshua was 12 years of age and growing rapidly when he started complaining of acute pains in his legs. He was taken first to the doctor's surgery then after a bit of a panic, quickly on to the hospital. The Family Doctor was of the opinion that his condition was very serious. X-rays were taken and a week later a consultant in the local hospital explained, with the help of the X-ray pictures, that this was simply a matter of growing pains. Joshua's body was finding it difficult to keep up with the growth of his bones. It was fascinating to look at the X-rays and to see the clear growth of new bone even in one week!

The church of Jesus Christ, the Body of Christ, frequently experiences growing pains. The transition that Ezekiel saw in his vision of the dry bones becoming a mighty army was growth of gigantic proportions:

> So I prophesied as I was commanded. And as I was prophesying, there was a noise, a rattling sound, and the bones came together, bone to bone. I looked, and tendons and flesh appeared on them and skin covered them, but there was no breath in them.
>
> Then he said to me, 'Prophesy to the breath; prophesy, son of man, and say to it, "This is what the Sovereign LORD says: Come from the four winds, O breath, and breathe into these slain, that they may live."' So I prophesied as he commanded me, and breath entered them; they came to life and stood up on their feet – a vast army.
> Ezekiel 37:7–10

Sometimes the structures of a church can no longer bear the new growth and changes have to be made. We have discovered in previous chapters that in order for us to function properly within the Body of Christ we need to be properly joined to the Body. A body made up of disconnected limbs is really no body at all but when God's people, as one body, are committed to one another and relating in love, then it is possible for each part to fulfill its nature and calling. However, the body must then learn to grow and develop together in love.

The church of Jesus Christ has an unchanging message but the ways of 'being church' have to be constantly under review. Eddie Gibbs and Ian Coffey in their book *Church Next* analyze some church models and propose nine areas in which the church will need to transform to be biblically true to its message. They identify these areas as 'major storm centers' through which churches have to navigate. Among the nine areas, all of which are vital, the first area is foundational to all the others. It is a call to stop living in the past and to engage with the present. Churches that refuse to move from their 'glorious past' invariably die. The church is a missionary movement, and this implies:

- The re-allocation of resources to facilitate experimentation;
- The development of pilot projects;
- The consolidation of gain;
- The humble spirit of pilgrim adventurers who take God at his word.

The truth is that not only many Christians but also many leaders in the church today are reeling from the pace of change, not only in society, but within the church itself.

The question is: What are the best structures to cope with the church of the twenty-first century?

Once again it is to the scriptures that we look for our answer. Ours is an unchanging God and the principles revealed in scripture are timeless and are never outmoded in the light of passing ecclesiastical expediency.

Leadership in the New Testament

It is clear from the New Testament that the first effects of the preaching of the gospel were that many people were converted. The apostles were concerned with evangelism and discipleship. As we have already seen people with suitable abilities were appointed to oversee situations as they arose as in Acts chapter 6.

Christ is the sole head of the church. In all things he is the ultimate authority over the church which he purchased with his own blood and called into being by the power of his Spirit. Having said that, we must go on to define Christ's provision for the continuance, guidance and oversight of the church.

In the historical, visible beginnings of the church, the only people who exercised any authority or gave care to the believers were the Apostles. The first Apostles were 'the Twelve' – Jesus' original disciples. The first chapter of the Acts of the Apostles tells us about their function and qualifications. Their function was to witness to the resurrection of Jesus Christ. Their qualification was they had been with the Lord Jesus during his ministry (Acts 1:21–22). However, the New Testament refers also to other apostles who clearly did not meet this qualification but were stilled called 'apostles'. This was a considerably larger group which included Epaphroditus in the Philippian church, Barnabas and Paul sent out by the church at Antioch, and Andronicus and Junias who are described in Romans 16 as 'outstanding among the apostles'.

A missionary situation, creating new churches, needed a development of leadership. The expanding situation in Jerusalem and further afield caused the responsibilities to be too much for the Apostles and so in Acts chapter 6 we read of seven disciples being appointed to serve in the local church. In Acts

11:30 we read that elders were functioning in Judea, whilst in Acts 14:23 Paul and Barnabas appointed elders in 'every church' before they returned to Antioch at the end of their first missionary journey. It is also clear from Acts 15:2 that elders were functioning in the Jerusalem church.

Whilst the Apostles were God's gift for the foundation and initial care of the churches, a structure was emerging for the continuing care, health and growth of the Body of Christ through the ages. It is my conviction that for local churches to flourish and for new churches to be planted there needs to be a rediscovery of the apostolic and prophetic ministries evidently present in the New Testament. I have been pleased to be identified, since its inception, with Mainstream, a Word and Spirit network of missionary leaders and churches. It continues to pioneer thinking and promote prayer towards this end. I commend its publications which will assist thinking and working through the roles of trans-local ministries.

However, the scope of this book is seeing the renewal of healthy local churches that will impact their communities in this generation. So what follows is limited to the local church.

Leadership is God's gift to the church and he has the responsibility of appointing it and it is solemnly accountable to him. My purpose now is to examine leadership roles within the local church with reference to the relationships between ministers, elders and deacons.

The New Testament uses four terms when referring to leaders. They are 'elder', 'bishop', 'pastor' and 'deacon'. But we are faced with a problem. It would make our understanding easier if all the words represented distinct roles or offices within the first-century church which we could then examine with the intention of reproducing them in the twenty-first-century church. We cannot do this for two reasons.

First, the New Testament describes a rapidly changing situation which does not provide us with a static, unchanging norm for us to imitate. Rather, when the pastoral epistles were written, the emphasis was not on office or structure but on character and qualifications.

Secondly, the terms 'elder' and 'bishop' were synonymous. This conclusion is based on Acts 20:17, 28; 1 Timothy 3:1; 5:17 and Titus 1:5ff. With this in mind it should be helpful to look at the terms used, their background, meaning and some of the functions attached to them.

The word 'elder' does not constitute an official title but simply means 'one who has matured'. However, this does not necessarily mean that an elder has to be an older person. Being old does not guarantee maturity and neither does being young necessarily imply immaturity. Clearly Timothy was appointed as an elder in the church at Ephesus when he was a young man and so we find Paul encouraging him, 'Don't let anyone look down on you because you are young' (1 Timothy 4:12).

'Elder' was a Jewish title derived from the leadership in the synagogue. In the Old Testament elders were selected for their wisdom, piety and integrity (Exodus 18; Deuteronomy 1). They acted as judges in disputes and were entrusted with the law, being charged to read it to the people (Deuteronomy 31:9–13).

In the New Testament we find elders present in the church in Jerusalem and they are regarded as those competent to judge between right and wrong (Acts 15:2; 16:4). Elders direct the affairs of the church where they are appointed and have a responsibility to teach and preach (1 Timothy 5:17). On the basis of their responsibilities, outlined and described in the New Testament, it is difficult to distinguish them from the bishops and oversees we consider next.

The word 'bishop' is also used in the New Testament in reference to leaders. It means 'overseer' or 'guardian' and conveys the idea of spiritual oversight. This word comes from the background of secular Greek culture.

The bishops were those appointed by the emperors to govern captured or newly-founded city states. The bishop was responsible to the emperor, but oversight was delegated to him. He functioned as a commissioner, regulating the affairs of the new colony or acquisition. 'Episkopos' (bishop) therefore suggested two ideas to the First Century Greek mind: responsibility to a superior power, and an introduction to a new order of things.[30]

Since the early church contained a growing population of Gentile converts, this Greek term was used to convey some of the ideas inherent in the biblical concept of leadership. To be a bishop involved exercising responsibility for the welfare, spiritual or otherwise, of others. This presents us with another challenge, for such a responsibility belonged not exclusively to one individual but to the whole church fellowship. In fact the term is rarely applied to the office of one person in the New Testament. The actual word only appears five times. 'We never find a presbyter in the singular in the New Testament. He is always a member of the team.'[31]

The spirit of the overseer is exercised by Paul and Barnabas as they return to care for their converts (Acts 15:36). The work of the Christian overseer is based on that of the Lord Jesus Christ (1 Peter 2:25). 'Titles of office in the New Testament are essentially titles that apply to Christ in the first place'.[32] There was reluctance in the New Testament to use this word, as applying to one person, because all Christians are to demonstrate loving concern and care each other.

It is against this background of the responsibility of the whole fellowship and the caring nature of our Lord's ministry, that the church proceeded to call or appoint overseers or bishops. The major concern of the young church was to see disciples appointed who were people of quality and good character. They were to be guardians of the faith and to teach sound doctrine. In this way

Christians would be preserved from error and established in the faith (1 Timothy 4:16; 6:20; 2 Timothy 4:2; Titus 1:9).

There is never a hint of domination or control in the appointment or the exercise of these ministries but rather servant leadership is modeled.

The third word, 'pastor', is used in the New Testament to bring out a completely different nuance to leadership. Its normal meaning is 'shepherd' and comes from the agricultural setting of the day. It pictures the shepherd caring for his flock and therefore emphasizes the care, protection and leadership of the pastor for his people.

As a shepherd the pastor is present not to dominate or interfere, but to guard and preserve, particularly in the realm of revealed truth.

Some scholars equate the three terms (elder, bishop and pastor) as referring to the same leadership office, but each term communicates different meanings or nuances to various audiences. John MacArthur distinguishes between these three terms when he says, 'Elder emphasises who the man is, bishop speaks of what he does, and pastor deals with his attitude and character. All three terms are used of the same church leaders, and all three identify those who feed and lead the church. Yet each term has a unique emphasis.'[xxxiii]

The fourth word, 'deacon', is used quite regularly in the New Testament. In Greek circles, outside the Christian church, the idea of service and the servant were common, though not regarded very highly. A servant was one who waited at tables, particularly at cultic meals, cared for household needs or worked for the good of the community. Such service, though present in early Judaism, was also considered to be beneath the dignity of a free man. Though Jews accepted responsibilities to the poor, they made provision through almsgiving, not service. Synagogues, in the Diaspora, often set up a council of seven persons to administer common meals and alms distribution.

The prominence given in the New Testament to the servant and service stands in marked contrast. Though most translations of the New Testament actually use the word 'deacon' only in Philippians 1:1 and four times in 1 Timothy 3, the original Greek word *diakonos* occurs 30 times and the words 'to minister' or 'ministry' occur a further 70 times. Through the clear identification of Jesus Christ as the servant of humanity (Mark 10:45), the person of the servant, and the activity of serving, are raised to the highest possible dignity. To serve and care for one's fellow human beings and their needs, far from being degrading functions, are essential to a Christian's calling and privilege (John 13:12–17).

It is sometimes assumed that the appointment of the 'seven' to 'serve tables' in Acts 6 is the formal institution of the office of deacon. The seven are never called deacons but the verb 'deaconing' is used. Paul claims to be a servant (deacon) of the gospel (Ephesians 3:7) and a servant through whom the Corinthian Christians had come to faith (1 Corinthians 3:5). Nevertheless, in the light of the obvious parallel between synagogue practice in the Diaspora and what is recorded in Acts 6, it is difficult to reject the idea that here was at least an embryonic diaconate. We should not be surprised to detect the gradual appearance on the scene of specific Christians described as 'deacons' (Philippians 1:1; 1 Timothy 3:8–13).

What, then, was the particular responsibility of the deacon as distinct from the 'deaconing' or 'serving' expected of all those who follow Jesus, the perfect pattern of servanthood? Another look at the Acts 6 incident may point to a possible answer.

> The significance lies…not in the institution of an order in the ministerial hierarchy, but of the first example of that delegation of administrative and social responsibilities to those of appropriate character and gifts, which was to become typical of the Gentile church, and the recognition of such duties as part of the ministry of Christ.[34]

It has been suggested that elders supervise and deacons serve but this misses the point: both offices are servant leadership roles. In some churches elders have a leadership role in the pastoral and spiritual affairs of the church while the deacons are seen to be responsible for the more practical affairs in church life.

> However the distinction between the 'spiritual' and the 'practical' cannot easily be maintained – the handling of money, for instance, normally seen as a diaconal responsibility, calls for a high degree of spirituality! On the other hand, it is true to say that in some churches where there are no elders, although in theory the deacons are responsible for overseeing both the spiritual and practical affairs of the church's life, time and again the practical concerns override the spiritual concerns.[35]

The qualifications listed in 1 Timothy 3 are particularly appropriate for those who worked in the sensitive areas of care, finance and administration and also served at the love feast where charity was frequently administered. Despite the paucity of New Testament evidence about their function, it seems most likely that the responsibilities of deacons lay in the areas of the social welfare of the church and the administration of its material resources.

In summary, it is possible to see two influences emerging in the appointment of individuals in the early church to the specific office of deacon. The first is the felt need for people who can be recognized as permanent sources of help and service in the fellowship of the church. The second is the recognition that there was need in the church for a serving office as distinct from the specific leadership office of the bishops or overseers.

Ministry Today

The normative New Testament picture is, therefore, one of a two-fold local ministry of elders (including pastors) and deacons. Other ministries existed in the churches. As well as apostles, there were 'prophets… teachers…workers of miracles…those having gifts of healing, those able to help others, those with gifts of administration, and those speaking in different kinds of tongues' (1 Corinthians 12:28). Such individuals, however, might or might not exist in any particular local church but were usually present in trans-local situations. Elders, by contrast, were supposed to be present in every church (Acts 14:23, Titus 1:5) and deacons were bracketed with these overseers in the greeting in Philippians 1:1. Their standing did not depend solely on their reception of the gifts of the Spirit, but also on their recognition by the church as individuals set apart for permanent responsibil-ities. The eldership and diaconate were church offices in a sense that other roles were not. Historically, therefore, most Christian churches have seen no reason to create posts for apostles, prophets, and teachers, but that position is being challenged today with the emergence of the new churches and the phenomenal growth of Pentecostal churches.

Baptists, whose experience of church I am most acquainted with, have seen no justification for the familiar distinction between ministers and elders. The traditional Presbyterian case for differentiating between teaching elders (ministers) and ruling elders (plain elders) rested on one verse, 1 Timothy 5:17. This verse does reveal that there were elders in the early church who were specialist preachers and teachers, but there is no ground for supposing they formed a separate class of elders from those charged with 'ruling'. Nowhere else is there a hint of two categories of elder; on the contrary, being over the congregation and admonishing it are expressly linked (1 Thessalonians 5:12). Consequently, among Baptists, ministers have always been regarded as elders. During the eighteenth century the term 'minister' almost entirely superseded 'elder', but the office remained the same. Part-time elders have sometimes been ordained, and there have been full-time elders without secular employment. This is exactly as it should be, for there is no biblical justification for distinguishing between ministers and elders. Whether full- or part-time, ordained or 'lay', they hold the same responsibilities. Ministers, in New Testament terms, are elders – no more, no less.

The valid distinction, as we have seen, is between the elder and the deacon. It is evident, from the similarity of the qualifications for the two offices in 1 Timothy 3, that the offices are closely allied, but it is equally evident from the fact that the qualifications are listed separately that the positions were in some sense different. It has been suggested that the elder was distinguished by being a teacher representing the church universal in the local church, whereas the deacon was only a local officer. Both, on this view, shared the same work of pastoral ministry. But this idea is open to serious doubt.

In applying these principles to the church in the twenty-first century we face many difficulties and in writing this book I am aware that some readers may be in churches with 30 members, others in churches with 300, or even a few with 3,000 members. The dynamics and practice of leading churches of different sizes are very different. We therefore have to contextualize the principles so that they are relevant to each church.

Plurality of Leadership

My philosophy of leadership has developed over the past 40 years. First, it involves setting up a plurality of leadership in the local church incorporating these ministries. Each leader is God's gift to the church. By exercising plurality of leaders, the local church does not become too dependent on the personality and gifts of one individual (the pastor). Furthermore the task of 'equipping the saints' is spread over the whole leadership team (the elders and deacons), resulting in a healthier, more balanced body of believers.

With a membership exceeding 300, my last pastoral charge created a Leadership Council where each elder or deacon was appointed to fulfill a particular task. There were nine areas of responsibilities and we operated on the 'heads of department' principle. It worked well. The Leadership Council met once a month but each working group had a mandate to do the work they were responsible for within the annually agreed budget!

All the working groups were responsible for and accountable to the church meeting via the Leadership Council for all areas detailed below:

• Pastoral: Responsibility for the oversight of membership, straying sheep, pastoral care, special needs, fellowship groups, nurture/discipleship, counseling, prayer ministry, students, ladies' work, men's work, luncheon club, prayer, home communion, sick visiting, magazine, inter-church relationships, training, social events, over 21s, dedications/cradle roll and babysitting scheme.

• Worship services: Responsibility for all aspects of Sunday worship including preaching, services format, music, welcome, stewarding, refreshments, communion, prayer ministry, audio/visual, tape ministry, drama, readers, prayer, other 'special' occasions, fire drill and flowers.

• Children and young people: Responsibility for Sunday and weekday programs for children and young people to 21 years of age, including youth weekends, schools work, discipleship (YP), playgroup, toddlers' group, training teachers and Safe to Grow.

• Global mission: Responsibility for stimulating interest and action in supporting mission both in the UK and overseas, including recognition of candidates for training and short-term mission and the support of students in training and missionaries sent out from our local church. Responsibilities also include the oversight of our relationships with the Baptist Missionary Society

(BMS) World Mission, Baptist Union of Great Britain (BUGB), Home Mission, Tearfund, Christian Aid, Tools With A Mission, and of our twinning arrangements with Poland and our missionary links with Croatia and Romania.

• Evangelism/Social action: Responsibility for the outreach program of the church including creative methods of sharing the Good News: local events, open air meetings, Jesus Video Project, Alpha Course, prayer cover for events, prayer walking, training for evangelism, Home Access, and Christmas gifts; prayerfully discovering creative methods of local action to meet needs; working with Penarth CYTUN Social Justice Group[xxxvi] to ensure that there is Christian input into relevant local, national and international issues; ensuring input from our church on concerns outside the remit of the CYTUN Group.

• Administration: Responsibility for all general adminis-tration matters of the church including liaison with BUGB, church correspondence, distribution of information, mainte-nance of membership roll and the list of the 'Friends of Tabernacle', trust and constitutional matters, and annotated agenda and minutes of the church meeting.

• Center Organizing Group: Responsibility for liaison with the caretaker, all staff matters, use of church center, repro-graphics, bookstall, publicity, security, catering, health and safety matters and the production of the Annual Report; mainte-nance, repair and improvements to all church property; oversight of all equipment, maintenance program, special projects and fire safety matters.

• Finance: Responsibility for all matters pertaining to income and expenditure and on financial matters generally: preparing and presenting budgets annually; promoting and administering covenants and Gift Aid; ensuring the provision of up-to-date accounts and arranging audit; administering loans, insurance and the church payroll; other financial dealings of the church.

These are the leaders appointed to help the church function

structurally. But there are, and must be, other leaders appointed to an equally vital role, namely the small group leaders (or house group or cell leaders, as others may call them). These leaders are appointed to enable the Ephesians 4:12 principle to work, whereby leaders are provided by God to equip the saints for the work of ministry.

As stated in chapter 8, 'To Cell or Not to Cell', our small group leaders meet together once every three months. This has become an increasingly important gathering as are the training courses which facilitate in-service training. The appointment of joint leaders and use of the gifts of the members of the group cannot be overstated. The small groups are themselves a place of development of gifts and the place where leaders emerge.

There is, I believe, a crisis of epic proportions in leadership today in the church and in the world. It is imperative that the church goes back to the Bible and seeks to produce anointed leaders in a biblical manner with discipline, accountability and oversight. Otherwise the church will die for lack of leadership and remain in the valley of dry bones.

Chapter 12

'Like a Mighty Army Moves the Church of God'

'Up and out! Up and out!' yelled our company staff sergeant at Boys' Brigade Battalion Camp. Ron was a small man but a giant of a motivator. He wanted our company to win the Best Tent Competition every day. As soon as reveille sounded he was outside our bell tent undoing the toggles and with one stride was in the center of the tent tapping the pole with his 'swagger' stick. We usually responded immediately as we knew if we didn't, a Wellington boot would be coming our way.

I have often heard those words in the intervening years: 'Up and out!' The phrase seems to have a divine authority about it.

Since my conversion as a boy, I have been constrained by the love of Christ to tell what God has done in Christ. My friends and I started a Christian Union at our secondary school. We were only 14 years of age but, with the encouragement of a new teacher, our group became the means by which a number of school friends started on the road of Christian discipleship.

The Boys' Brigade (BB) played an important part in my own discipling. It was therefore very significant that my 'harvesting' as a young evangelist began at a Boys' Brigade Battalion Camp. It was August 1971 in Swanage, Dorset. As chaplain I had responsibilities for speaking each morning and presiding at evening prayers. The Holy Spirit was present in a supernatural way and 33 boys and seven officers professed faith. The camp secretary wrote to me on our return, expressing gratitude for what I had allowed the Holy Spirit to do through me. He added, 'I feel sure that the work started at the 1971 Battalion Camp will continue. In the years which may lie ahead the BB and churches in Cardiff will reap an even greater harvest.' That was to prove prophetic. During the next three years no fewer than 1,000 young people were to profess faith in the Cardiff area through the ministry of a small group of people that became known as the Cardiff Youth Committee for Local Evangelism.

One of the significant lessons learnt from what can only be described as a sovereign work of God was the way in which those young people were followed up and nurtured.

Making Disciples

On my return from camp I wrote to the leaders of the churches from which those boys and young men had come. Generally speaking, the ministers and church leaders were thrilled and committed themselves to nurturing them. However, from other ministers there was a sense of cynicism and no commitment to continuing the work of making disciples.

We therefore took it upon ourselves after every evangelistic initiative (and there were many, usually of the coffee bar nature) to organize a series of discipleship classes. Colleagues in the ministry at that time included Rev. Stuart Ryce-Davies of Rhiwbina Baptist Church and Rev. Mervyn Morgan who had planted Emmanuel Baptist Church, Gabalfa, Cardiff. They worked tirelessly with the committed purpose of making disciples of those who had committed their lives to Christ.

We wrote our own discipleship material and led sessions that covered foundational subjects including:

- What is a disciple?
- Four disciplines: Bible reading, prayer, fellowship, witness
- God and the universe
- The person and work of Jesus Christ
- How to be filled with the Holy Spirit
- Christian security: how you can be sure you are a Christian
- Christian baptism

- Church membership

Those were remarkable days and memorable occasions. It is not insignificant that today more than a few of those young people are leaders in the Christian church active around the world.

I felt at that time that I was a part of a church that was "Like a mighty army moves the church of God"; the title of this chapter which is taken from the hymn 'Onward Christian Soldiers" by Sabine Baring-Gould (1834-1924)

Over 30 years on, the passion is still burning brightly in my heart to make disciples. It was nearly 2,000 years ago, however, that the risen Lord Jesus Christ commissioned his disciples to 'go and make disciples of all nations, baptizing them in the name of the Father and of the Son and of the Holy Spirit, and teaching them to obey everything I have commanded you. And surely I am with you always, to the very end of the age' (Matthew 28:19–20). Our Lord had a vision of his followers being involved in making the Good News known so that disciples would be made and God's Kingdom established on the earth. The words of that commission have never been withdrawn and the vision for winning the world for Jesus Christ is still as clear now as when the Savior first presented it. The question must be asked: Are we playing our part?

Obey the Great Commission with Christ's Power
Before the Great Commission was given, Jesus assured his disciples, 'All authority in heaven and on earth has been given to me' (Matthew 28:18). This means that all the powers of heaven, earth and hell are under the authority of the risen Christ. Luke's account of Jesus' last words reads like this: 'But you will receive power when the Holy Spirit comes on you; and you will be my witnesses in Jerusalem and in all Judea and Samaria, and to the

ends of the earth' (Acts 1:8). Instead of 'power' we could use the word 'dynamite'. As we have observed, on the Day of Pentecost there was plenty of spiritual dynamite in evidence. The same dynamic power is available today. We are not fighting for victory, but from victory. We have to enter into the victory that Christ won on Calvary. The powers of darkness were defeated there. The resurrection was the sign that all authority truly does belong to the Lord Jesus Christ. By the Holy Spirit he releases that power in us and through us.

First-century disciples took these words so seriously that in a little over 33 years the whole of the then known world had been evangelized. They knew that to be under the authority of the risen Christ was to be able to experience divine power and to overcome devilish power.

Divine power

As we walk through the pages of the Acts of the Apostles, time after time we see the power of the risen Christ made manifest through ordinary people.

Peter and John, when confronted by the lame man outside the temple in Jerusalem, saw the real need of this beggar and Peter said, 'Silver or gold I do not have, but what I have I give to you. In the name of Jesus Christ of Nazareth, walk' (Acts 3:6). At the mention of the name of Jesus Christ, divine power was released and the man walked.

Let us not miss the significance of signs and wonders in relationship to evangelistic enterprises. Jesus said it would be like this:

> And these signs will accompany those who believe: In my name they will drive out demons; they will speak in new tongues; they will pick up snakes with their hands; and when they drink deadly poisons, it will not hurt them at all; they will place their hands on sick people, and they will get well.

Mark 16:17–18

We do not see many miracles performed in 'developed' countries but I have seen far more physical healings during evangelistic work than I have seen in pastoral situations. We ought not to be surprised. The miracles are often signs to an unbelieving world and are means of gathering many into the Kingdom of God.

It should go without saying that the greatest miracle is the salvation of souls. Another tragedy today is that believers fail to recognize and feel the deep and desperate spiritual need of men and women who are without Christ.

The famous British preacher Roland Hill, addressing the people of Wootton during one of his pastorates, exclaimed,

> Because I am in earnest in my preaching men call me an enthusiast, a fanatic. When I first came to this part of the country I was walking on that hill and saw a great gravel pit fall in and bury three human beings alive. I lifted up my voice for help so loudly that I was heard in the town below at a distance of nearly a mile. Help came and two of the sufferers were rescued. No one called me a fanatic that day; yet when I see eternal destruction ready to fall on poor sinners and I call upon them to escape men dare to call me an enthusiast and a fanatic. How little they know of the fearfulness of my responsibility to men!

Devilish power

Those early disciples recognized that 'our struggle is not against flesh and blood, but against the rulers, against the authorities, against the powers of this dark world and against the spiritual forces of evil in the heavenly realms' (Ephesians 6:12). They declared, 'The weapons we fight with are not the weapons of the world. On the contrary, they have divine power to demolish strongholds' (2 Corinthians 10:4). It was with confidence that they could say, 'Submit yourselves, then, to God. Resist the devil, and he will flee from you' (James 4:7).

The fact that they knew how to resist the devil is again illustrated for us in the Acts of the Apostles. The Apostle Paul was opposed by Elymas, the sorcerer.

> Then...Paul, filled with the Holy Spirit, looked straight at Elymas and said, 'You are a child of the devil and an enemy of everything that is right! You are full of all kinds of deceit and trickery. Will you never stop perverting the right ways of the Lord? Now the hand of the Lord is against you. You are going to be blind, and for a time you will be unable to see the light of the sun.'
>
> Immediately mist and darkness came over him, and he groped about, seeking someone to lead him by the hand.
> Acts 13:9–11

If we are to obey the Great Commission, we must experience the divine power and know how to overcome devilish power.

Most Christians are inwardly terrified about engaging in personal witness to what God has done for us in Christ. Many of us cover up with a brave smile but underneath it lies sheer panic. Many reasons could be given for this fear but the principal one, in my opinion, is the fact that we are not filled with the Holy Spirit and not learning to flow in his power. The church is responsible for training its disciples to give away their faith and to send them out to do so in the power of the Holy Spirit.

Obey the Great Commission with Christ's Program

'Go and make disciples of all nations, baptizing them in the name of the Father and of the Son and of the Holy Spirit, and teaching them to obey everything I have commanded you. And surely I am with you always, to the very end of the age' (Matthew 28:19–20). The step by step program is so simple.

Step 1: 'Go and make disciples'

The fact that we are a minority grouping in the community is nothing new. But it is equally a fact that churches that are growing through evangelism are reaching unchurched people. Forrest Gump said it well (in the 1994 film of the same name):

Lieutenant Dan: 'Have you found Jesus yet, Gump?'
Gump: 'I didn't know we were supposed to be looking for him, sir.'[37]

"One of the major obstacles to effective evangelism today is that people no longer hear the Good News of Jesus Christ as news that is good. What the church usually has to say is seldom perceived as newsworthy, and it is often presented in a way that makes it sound bad or unimportant.

The fact that the gospel is essentially about Jesus Christ means it really is news that is good for everyone. But how can we get people to listen? First, we need to know what the Good News consists of and how it relates to what non-Christians understand and know about God.

Secondly, we need to be able to tell others what the Good News means to us. We need to share our good news of what has happened to us through our faith in Jesus Christ".[38] We need to know how God has changed our lives and to be able to share the testimonies of our experience as committed Christians.

Peter put it well:

In your hearts set apart Christ as Lord. Always be prepared to give an answer to everyone who asks you to give the reason for the hope that you have. But do this with gentleness and respect, keeping a clear conscience, so that those who speak maliciously against your good behavior in Christ may be ashamed of their slander.
1 Peter 3:15–16

The best way for any church to reach its community is by helping its disciples tell their own story of what God has done for them. There is a great example for us to study in Acts 26:1–29. Notice the transition from one part of Paul's testimony to the other. The 'before', 'how' and 'since' elements are very distinct and could be noted in the spaces below.

Think about those things that characterize the life of Paul before and since he met Jesus. For the 'how' section, simply record the details of his conversion on the road to Damascus. Consider the changes in his life that must have taken place. These extra passages may prove helpful: Acts 9:1–22; 22:3–21; Philippians 3:3–16.

Write down your discoveries about Paul's testimony:

Before Paul met Jesus his life was (Acts 26:1–11)

....
....
....
....

How he met Jesus (Acts 26:12–18)

....
....
....
....

Since he met Jesus (Acts 26:19–32)

....
....
....
....

Of course, before being able to tell your story, you've got to win a hearing by being sincerely interested in people. Jesus was a friend of sinners and often met with them (Luke 15:1–2). Instead of having one consuming drive to press home the verbal witness, win the confidence of people by being interested in them. Let them tell you their problems, heartaches and concerns. Ask them what they feel is their greatest need. Just being a good listener will open many doors. This may mean that you get involved a lot more deeply into the lives and problems of people. In the long run you will have a more sympathetic individual, with whom you can share Christ, and they will soon be asking you to explain what makes you so different.

Now prepare to tell your story. Try to remember the things you felt were wrong, or were problems in your life, before you became a Christian – possibly such things as selfishness, immorality, dishonesty, hypocrisy, fear, pride, lack of purpose, loneliness, bad language and hatred, to name but a few! Fill in the first part, 'Before I met Jesus my life was...', with some of those things you remember.

Before I met Jesus my life was...

....
....
....
....

How did you decide to follow Jesus? Through going to church, going to a youth camp, attending an evangelistic meeting, reading the Bible, listening to a Christian friend or relative, or seeing a film? Did you grow up in a Christian home and have you been a follower of Jesus for as long as you can remember? Or did you come to him in some other way? Fill in the second part, 'How I met Jesus...' with your way.

How I met Jesus...

....
....
....
....

What are the benefits of being a Christian? You might suggest such things as being a member of God's family, knowing forgiveness, having a purpose for living, going to heaven, receiving strength in difficult times or the fellowship of other Christians. Can you think of others?

How do these benefits change the unpleasant things that were in your life before you met Jesus? Fill in the third and final part of your story, 'Since I met Jesus...' with the changes in your life.

Since I met Jesus...

....

....

....

....

Now think of those people you can tell your story to and pray that you will be better witnesses as you share the Good News with others.

However, words are not enough on their own. To be a 'witness' to the Good News implies more than just giving a verbal testimony. The word 'witness' might also be translated 'martyr'. Having the characteristics of a martyr is rare in these days but it is the New Testament standard for those who call themselves disciples. So many people call themselves witnesses but are not honest. Deep down in their hearts they know they are not martyrs for Jesus Christ. A martyr is not made by death but is discovered at death. Unless a person is a living martyr, he can never be a dying one. The sin of hypocrisy and inconsistency on the part of Christians has been a stumbling block to the unconverted from the very beginning.

Mark Twain blamed the inconsistencies of Christian leaders for his turning away from the Christian faith. As he grew up, he knew elders and deacons who owned slaves and abused them. He heard men using foul language and saw them practice dishonesty during the working week after speaking piously in church on Sunday. Although he saw genuine love for the Lord Jesus in some people, including his mother and his wife, he was so disturbed by the bad teaching and poor example of church leaders that he became bitter towards the things of God. If the church is to make disciples it will do so because Christians are living out lives that are evidently different from those of non-Christians.

Step 2: 'Baptize them in the name of the Father, Son and Holy Spirit'

Once people have been introduced to the Lord Jesus Christ they are to be encouraged to be baptized as a public pledge of loyalty to Christ and the church. The New Testament knows nothing of spiritual gypsies. The first believers belonged to a local gathering of Christians and were accountable to one another.

This is a major problem for the church of the twenty-first century. Organized Christianity is a real put-off so is it any wonder that we have difficulty trying to get people to sign up to belong in a committed way? The situation is so bad that many people have given up and opted out of church life altogether.

Others, frustrated by the apparent irrelevance of the church as they know it, are attempting to establish alternative methods of being church. There are cyber-churches, café churches, pub churches, midweek churches. These are early days so we must neither write them off nor jump on the bandwagon. We need to wait on God and catch the wind of the Spirit. He is certainly stirring the next generation of Christianity in the UK and across Western culture.

I applaud every effort of the local churches to relate to the contemporary culture. What we must not do is to give up on the church. The church of Jesus Christ is still the instrument of the Kingdom of God.

It has always been a natural tendency to opt out of the responsibilities of discipleship when the going gets tough. The writer of the Hebrews exhorts, 'Let us not give up meeting together, as some are in the habit of doing, but let us encourage one another – and all the more as you see the Day approaching' (Hebrews 10:25).

It is essential that places are created where we have fellowship with one another and where we encounter and fellowship with God. As I said in Chapter 7, the coming of the Holy Spirit into the lives of the early Christians produced amongst them a spirit of oneness in unity that excelled anything previously experienced by the people of God. So unique was the sense of community that the New Testament writers had to create a word to describe it, the word *koinonia*. Unfortunately, like many other words in our language, fellowship has become debased. The word has become so devalued that it seldom means more than a nice get-together in church, followed by coffee and biscuits! Fellowship is one of the great words of the New Testament and we need to redeem it and restore to it the meaning that was once attached to it. I am convinced that for a church to be a healthy congregation it must discover once again the spirit of oneness and unity that marked the New Testament church.

Like it or not, the formation of local churches of this quality is part of God's program for the reaching of the world.

Step 3: 'Teach them to obey everything I have commanded you'

The Great Commission is not over when we get people to sign up to the local church. The making of disciples is a continuous program.

Any superficiality and ignorance in the life of the church is generally due to negligence of this vital step in the Lord's program. That is why I devoted a chapter to the value of small groups. Everyone serious about being a disciple of Jesus Christ must be committed to ongoing learning.

Obey the Great Commission with Christ's Presence

'Surely I am with you always, to the very end of the age' (Matthew 28:19–20). It is only as we commit ourselves to obeying the Great Commission that we know the manifestation of the presence of Christ with us. Mark ended his Gospel with this lovely footnote: 'Then the disciples went out and preached everywhere, and the Lord worked with them and confirmed his word by the signs that accompanied it' (Mark 16:20).

There are some sad words at the close of Paul's last letter to Timothy. Nearing the close of his ministry he tells how he feels he has been forsaken by everyone but then adds, 'The Lord stood at my side and gave me strength so that through me the message might be fully proclaimed and all the Gentiles might hear it.' (2 Timothy 4:17). I have certainly felt like that and have known those moments when I have heard the whisper, 'Never will I leave you; never will I forsake you. So…say with confidence, "The Lord is my helper; I will not be afraid"' (Hebrews 13:5–6).

When we commit ourselves to obeying the Great Commission we can be assured not only of his presence but also the proof of his presence: 'Then the disciples went out and preached everywhere and the Lord worked with them and confirmed his word by the signs that accompanied it' (Mark 16:20). As it was for Jesus, so we might expect it to be for us. The acid test of our effectiveness in the making of disciples is seen in the lives of transformed individuals and communities.

How We Work

The implications of the Great Commission in the local church will call for that church to have a period of waiting on God to guide them in the development of a strategy that will work for them.

Reference has been made to going to where the people are and employing appropriate methods for engaging them in their comfort zones even if they are not ours. However, most of the professions of faith made through my ministry have come through expository preaching with a sharp evangelistic edge. This presents another problem faced by the average pastor preacher: that of addressing congregations or audiences that do not constitute an evangelistic target. Therefore, whilst the Great Commission is to 'go', it is still appropriate for us to talk about how we get the outsider to come in. I believe there is a place for teaching and training disciples in the art of bringing people to a place where the Good News can be heard. There is no shortage of methods being suggested today.

Spontaneous evangelism
A survey in recent years on how people were helped to find a personal relationship with Jesus Christ showed the three top methods were:

- Through befriending
- Through the use of the home
- Through bringing non-Christians into a loving, praying, warm, worshiping church fellowship

Nine out of ten people who come to faith in Jesus Christ do so through a family member or a friend. The trouble is that we are so busy 'doing' church that we have insufficient time to spend with our unchurched friends.

I visited a church recently which, during the previous year, had experienced an influx of new people in their twenties and thirties. They had all come to faith through being invited to participate in the church's football and netball teams. Here the ordinary believer has an opportunity, under perfectly natural circumstances, to get to know people in the context of developing relationships, to talk about what makes them tick. This is sponta-neous evangelism, involving every Christian in their daily life. Spontaneous evangelism takes place through the 'networks' of relationships of believers.

Systematic evangelism
Systematic evangelism is that method of outreach organized collectively by the body of the church, using planned missions, events and services.

There is no lack of resources for this approach. There is a mountain of books on the mission of the church, there are conferences to motivate you, Bible weeks to renew your vision. Let me recommend two resources that will help you hit the road running.

The first is *50 Ways to Help Your Church Grow* by David Beer.[39] He answers the questions:

- How do you tread the path between vision and reality?
- How do you get all that unrealized potential out of the pew and into the street?
- How do you turn the tide from being a surviving church to a thriving church?

Rick Warren, author of *The Purpose Driven Church*, describes it as 'a book filled with hope! If put into practice, I believe it could bring about a mighty spiritual awakening that could touch every city and town and bring many to Christ'.

Another useful resource is *The Evangelism Toolkit: Seven Practical Ways to Reach Your Community*.[40] The seven practical ways are described as seven streams:

1. The Networking Method – looking at reaching your friends and acquaintances
2. The Samaritan Strategy – being a good neighbor in your area
3. Commitment To Kids – communicating the gospel to children

4. The Youth Challenge – mobilizing youth to reach their peers
5. The Caleb Approach – releasing the potentials of retired people
6. The Door-To-Door Plan – the systematic approach to door-to-door work
7. The Street Dynamic – taking the gospel to the streets

The Evangelism Toolkit has an introductory section, 'Ground Work', which looks at general principles to help us be effective in our evangelism projects. This includes sowing, reaping, prayer, goal setting and follow-up.

In the practical tools that form part of the kit there are extra notes on coordinating events, organizing guests' meetings, additional resources, Bible study notes and response forms. I believe every church ought to possess a copy of *The Evangelism Toolkit*.

Seeker Services

Seeker Services are proving an effective means of evangelism so it is not surprising that in recent days Christians in the UK have shown enormous interest in them.

Willow Creek Community Church, near Chicago, Illinois, which has provided the model many are copying, builds its work on the following principles:

1. All people matter to God; therefore they must matter to us.
2. Lost people need to be sought and found.
3. Evangelism and edification cannot effectively be done in the same service since the needs of the churched and the unchurched individual differ greatly.
4. Respect for the spiritual journey of the seeker must be communicated, allowed for and legitimized.
5. Seekers do not want to be embarrassed, singled out,

pressured or identified.

6. Excellence reflects the glory of God and has a positive effect on people.

Seeker Services are one element in the seven-step strategy designed to enable the unchurched to become 'fully devoted followers of Jesus Christ'. The strategy consists of:

1. Building authentic relationships
2. Sharing a verbal witness
3. Providing a service for seekers
4. Attendance at the new community services (for believers)
5. Participation in a small group
6. Involvement in ministry through the use of spiritual gifts
7. The exercise of stewardship

Divorced from these values and strategies, or similar ones, Seeker Services will be futile.

At Tabernacle, Penarth we experimented with Seeker Services and, whilst a couple of the steps were very successful, we did not find that the experience in any way improved on our existing strategy. That is the point: if you have a strategy that works in making disciples, stick with it for as long as it continues to work.

Never forget that the Great Commission is to 'go' and that as we go, the risen Lord journeys with us. It is through keeping in vital contact with him through prayer that we will be made aware of those strategies he wants us to adopt from time to time.

For a number of years we used the Jesus Video Project to great effect and saw a number of disciples established through that method. However, we saturated the area with the video until it came to a natural end. The Alpha Course is still part of our strategy and will remain so while people are interested in attending the groups.

Whatever kind of evangelism is used, it is invariably focused on specific areas of need amongst the people in the community and is built around relationships. We will provide examples in the next chapter, but first we have to capture the vision of the prophet Ezekiel as recorded in Ezekiel 37.

The Vision of the Great Commission
If we are going to sense the high and holy calling of witnessing to a world of desperate needs, we must have a vision of the general situation around us. The vision Ezekiel saw was a valley full of dry, scattered bones. It depicted the desolation, destitution and dereliction of Israel. Only as we have a similar vision of the world in which we live, will we be stirred into action. I am indebted to the late Rev Dr Stephen F. Olford for the insights and inspiration gained from his sermon *Vision for Outreach*".[41]

We have to recognize that men and women in the world today are spiritually lifeless, useless and hopeless.

• Spiritually lifeless: 'a valley...full of bones' (Ezekiel 37:1). The bones here speak of death.

Paul tells us that until the Holy Spirit quickens men and women into spiritual life, they are 'dead in trespasses and sins' (Ephesians 2:1 KJV). Though full of life physically, people can be dead spiritually.

• Spiritually useless: 'bones that were very dry' (Ezekiel 37:2).

We shall never be stirred into action until we realize that men and women around us are spiritually useless. As the Apostle wrote, 'they have together become worthless' (Romans 3:12).

• Spiritually hopeless: 'Our bones are dried up and our hope is gone; we are cut off' (Ezekiel 37:11).

The Bible speaks of unregenerate men and women as 'without hope and without God in the world' (Ephesians 2:12). The more we hear of uprising in the world – in spite of the attempts of our leaders to bring about peace in our time – the more we must be convinced of the hopelessness of the world's situation today.

Do you know the story of William Carey, considered by many

to be the father of the modern missionary movement? He lived in the eighteenth century, a cobbler by trade. He kept a map of the world on the wall of his workshop, so that he could pray for the nations of the world. He became burdened for a definite missionary outreach. When he shared his burden at a meeting of ministers, he was told by one of the senior ministers, 'Young man, sit down! When God wants to convert the heathen, he will do it without your help or mine.' But William Carey didn't let the fire of his enthusiasm be dampened by such a response and eventually left the shores of England to go to India where he engaged in pioneer mission work doing exploits for God. Do you share this vision for evangelism?

The prophet Ezekiel was told to prophesy to the bones and speak to them! Now that is preaching to corpses. If we take this literally, nothing could be more foolish or ridiculous than to preach to a bunch of dry bones. Indeed when God asked the question, 'Can these bones live?' Ezekiel's answer was 'O Sovereign LORD, you alone know' (Ezekiel 37:3). We can almost imagine the hesitancy on the part of the prophet as he considered the utter futility of the task.

No true preacher of the gospel is unfamiliar with such a situation but, humanly speaking, what is more difficult than to confront a world of lifeless, useless and hopeless men and women with a word of the gospel? Yet this is the clear obligation of the church. God has not promised to bless our theological systems, our superficial interpretations or our philosophical theorizing, but he has committed himself to bless the preaching of the pure Word of God. We can see the promise that he makes in Isaiah 55:11, the promise that his Word will not return to him empty but will accomplish what he desires and achieve what he purposes.

Only through such preaching will there be a coming together of these bones and a coming to life of these bones (Ezekiel 37:7). It is only the Word of God which can effect such miracles. The writer to the Hebrews describes the Word of God as 'living and active. Sharper than any double-edged sword, it penetrates even to dividing soul and Spirit, joints and marrow; it judges the thoughts and attitudes of the heart' (Hebrews 4:12). Yet the gospel of our Lord Jesus Christ is 'the power of God to salvation to everyone who believes' (Romans 1:16).

Preaching alone is insufficient; the prophet is encouraged to pray as well. 'Come...O breath, and breathe into these slain, that they may live' (Ezekiel 37:9). With the preaching there came a noise, a shaking, a coming together of bone with bone and even the appearance of sinews and skin, but the Word says, 'there was no breath in them' (37:8). Through preaching, people may be convinced of truth, but they are only corpses until the Spirit of God breathes upon them. Undoubtedly, this is why our Lord told his disciples to wait in Jerusalem until they were spiritually endued with power from on high (Luke 24:49). Then came the Day of Pentecost when there was a 'sound from heaven as of a rushing mighty wind' (Acts 2:2 KJV) and at once their preaching ministry was vitalized. As they spoke, dead men and women came to life.

This is still God's method of bringing the gospel to fulfillment. It is our obligation to see that we not only preach with urgency, but pray with fervency. We must be satisfied with nothing less than the outpouring of the Spirit of God. The world of lifeless, useless and hopeless men and women will never be changed unless the Holy Spirit breathes upon the preaching as well as upon the people.

An American preacher, William Lee, said,

It is not the arithmetic of our prayers, how many they are, nor the rhetoric of our prayers, how eloquent they are; nor the geometry of our prayers, how long they may be; nor the music of our prayers, how sweet our voice may be; nor the logic of our prayers, how argumentative they may be; nor the method of our prayers, how orderly they may be – which God cares for. Fervency of Spirit is that which avails much.[42]

These may be first-century methods but they still work in the twenty-first century. 'So I prophesied as he commanded me and breath entered them, they came to life and stood up on their feet – a vast army' (Ezekiel 37:10). Only when God breaks through from heaven are dead men and women vitalized, energized, mobilized and utilized.

• Vitalized: we read that 'they came to life' (37:10). Those corpses were animated, vitalized, brought back to life. The same thing can happen today as we preach the gospel in the power of the Holy Spirit. Our Lord assures us that 'It is the Spirit who gives life' (John 6:63 NKJV). Even a man like Nicodemus was blind in sin (he could not see the Kingdom of God); bound in sin (he could not enter the Kingdom of God); born in sin (he could not inherit the Kingdom of God) until he was quickened to life (born again).

A story is told in 'Our Daily Bread' of an English minister who visited missionaries in the South Sea Islands. He was profoundly impressed by the spiritual life of the students, by the art that decorated their buildings and by their personal cleanliness, but the highlight came as he was about to return to England. The girls lined up in two rows and sang enthusiastically, 'What a wonderful change in my life has been wrought since Jesus came into my heart!' He was very moved, but quite overwhelmed when one of the staff members whispered to him, 'Every one of those girls is either the daughter or granddaughter of a cannibal!

• Energized: 'They stood upon their feet' (37:10). Alongside a desire to see men and women quickened to life, we should be concerned that they are strengthened to stand for Christ and his church. Paul expressed this burden when writing to the Ephesian church saying that he was praying for them: 'I pray that [the Father] may strengthen you with power through his Spirit in your inner being, so that Christ may dwell in your hearts through faith. And I pray that you, being rooted and established in love, may have power' (Ephesians 3:14–17. Let us never forget that we are committed to pray earnestly for these babes in Christ that they may be strengthened by his Spirit to stand and to withstand.

• Mobilized: 'a vast army' (37:10). It is the work of the Holy Spirit to bring individual units into a whole. The Apostle Paul informs us, 'We were all baptized by one Spirit into one body' (1 Corinthians 12:13). Furthermore we are exhorted to 'keep the unity of the Spirit through the bond of peace' (Ephesians 4:3). God deliver us from being individualists or isolated units! May we rather be a unified whole – ' a vast army' (37:10). Only in such unity will there be strength.

• Utilized: 'I will put my Spirit in you and you will live, and I will settle you in your own land' (37:14). The ministry of the Holy Spirit is not only to vitalize, energize and mobilize but to utilize. Speaking to his disciples, the Lord Jesus said, 'You will receive power when the Holy Spirit comes on you; and you will be my witnesses' (Acts 1:8). There are no unwanted men and women in the church of Jesus Christ, for 'we are his workmanship, created in Christ Jesus for good works, which God prepared beforehand that we should walk in them' (Ephesians 2:10 NKJV). There is a place of witness for each one of us and we must see that we are led to it by the Holy Spirit.

Ever since the end of the Second World War, Japanese volunteers have been searching the island of Saipan for the bodies of soldiers killed there. Of the 40,000 to 50,000 Japanese soldiers and dependants believed to have died there, only half have been found. Because of that, there will be missions in the future looking for the dead. The church too has a mission for the dead. Men and women are 'dead in trespasses and sins' and the church must seek them out and proclaim life in the name of the Lord Jesus Christ. Then, like the bones of Ezekiel's vision, the dead shall live. Will you be a volunteer for Jesus and allow him to use your gifts in the mission to find lost men and women who are spiritually dead?

With this vision before us, may we go from one victory to another like an army – a vast army!

Chapter 13

An Army of Saboteurs

The late Malcolm Muggeridge once spoke about 'stay-behind agents', those individuals who stay behind after a nation has been defeated and gather together the 'underground' – an army of saboteurs. Muggeridge used this image from his own experience to remind us that as Christians we are here to explode the assumptions of people who are comfortable in the Kingdom of Self. Referring to some of the spiritual giants of church history he wrote,

> So I came to see them as God's spies, posted in actual or potential enemy-occupied territory, the enemy being, of course, in this particular case, the Devil. As it happens I was myself involved in espionage operations in the Second World War, when I served with MI6, the wartime version of the British Secret Service, or SIS. We had, for instance, what were known as stay-behind agents in German-occupied France, who were required to lie low until circumstances arose in which they could make themselves useful by collecting and transmitting intelligence, or organizing sabotage. While they were waiting to be activated, it was essential that they should make themselves inconspicuous by merging into the social and political scene, and, in their opinions and attitudes, echoing the current consensus.[43]

Jesus was a Master Saboteur; he not only became one of us, but also got behind the defenses of people and lovingly exposed them to the truth. The church of the twenty-first century needs to discover his secret.

Roger and Carol lived in a leafy suburb north of Cardiff. They surprised everyone by deciding to move home and buy a house in the docklands of Cardiff at a time when it was unfashionable to do so. They bought a terraced house a couple of hundred yards away from the church where I was the pastor. Their explanation for doing so was clear. As Jesus was incarnate in the world, so they felt they needed to flesh-up their discipleship in the community where they worshiped.

Over the past 25 years I have seen many other families make the same decision with the same motivation. In recent years several families moved from the beautiful rural Vale of Glamorgan to buy terraced houses near their church center in town. They did this not just to be able to walk to church but rather to be living witnesses to their neighbors. Churches are called to be incarnate in society. The pattern for our service has been laid down in the ministry of Jesus. 'As the Father sent me, I am sending you,' he said (John 20:21). Obedience to this command is costly. Sacrifice and suffering are inevitable consequences for the servant church even as they work for the Servant Christ. But healthy churches are willing to pay the price. They accept that the world is changing fast and they need to risk being part of what is happening in order to cooperate with it in the positive things and confront it in the negative things.

The Incarnation
The Word became flesh and blood,
and moved into the neighborhood.
We saw the glory with our own eyes,
the one-of-a-kind glory,
like Father, like Son,
generous inside and out,
true from start to finish.
John 1:14 *The Message*

What condescension, that the Almighty God should become a human being and live in our neighborhood!

> Think of yourselves the way Christ Jesus thought of himself. He had equal status with God but didn't think so much of himself that he had to cling to the advantages of that status no matter what. Not at all. When the time came, he set aside the privileges of deity and took on the status of a slave, became human! Having become human, he stayed human. It was an incredibly humbling process. He didn't claim special privileges. Instead, he lived a selfless, obedient life and then a selfless, obedient death – and the worst kind of death at that: the crucifixion.
>
> Philippians 2:5–8 *The Message*

Now that is humility of mind, heart and soul, and that is what we are called to imitate. St Augustine was asked, 'What is the first step to heaven?' He answered, 'Humility'. 'And the second step?' 'Humility'. 'And the third step?' 'Humility'.

Humility has been well defined as 'unconscious self-forgetfulness'. To this, disciples in the twenty-first century are still called. What our Lord Jesus Christ did in becoming incarnate we are to imitate; unconscious self-forgetfulness is a vital ingredient in accomplishing the lasting work of God. John the Baptist expressed it clearly when he said of Jesus, 'He must increase, but I must decrease' (John 3:30 KJV). Local churches have to learn how to engage with society effectively, using the places and vehicles of social encounter in order to embody and communicate grace and truth. There is no automatic connection between church and community so we must take such initiatives, building bridges that will penetrate the community in the hope that, by the grace of God, there will be encounters in which the human and divine will meet.

Intimate Involvement
At the beginning of the twenty-first century there are exciting opportunities and encouragements for local Christians to be intimately involved in local communities.

I believe there are two initial steps that every church needs to take. The first is to get to know your community and the second is to discover the need which God is calling you to address.

Know your community
There are, of course, different levels of community.

• The mini-community. This might be defined as the family unit, or our circle of friends; of course, the local church itself is a mini-community.

• The midi-community. This has been defined as a 'unit of residence'. Sometimes it is the parish boundary. When you are situated in a village or a town it is easily defined. However, when you live in a city, defining your midi-community is of vital importance. It may help to get a street map and simply look at the areas where your disciples live and work. It is this midi-community to which we are called for intimate involvement.

• The mega-community. This is the world. The television and the Internet gives us a sense of the mega-community. Everything today is global and Christians must accept a responsibility for the care of the whole universe.

We shall consider our responsibility to the world in the next chapter but for now we must think about the midi-community.

We must make time to develop friendships with our neighbors and work colleagues. We need to walk the streets with our eyes and our ears wide open. We all ask for more community policing but we need to be more concerned about community discipling. A friend involved for many years with the formation of Christian ministers has been calling for the end to patrol car pastors. We know what he means.

David Coffey, President of the Baptist World Alliance, wrote an article, 'So You Want to Build a Ship?' Amongst many challenging things, he said,

> To foster an apostolic church I suggest a modest change in our Baptist Union of Great Britain practice of ministerial settlement. When a minister receives a call to a new church the start of their public ministry of preaching, leading and pastoring should be delayed by up to three months. During that time they are encouraged to immerse themselves in the community of the church. They walk the streets and meet the people. They visit the statutory and voluntary agencies, all potential partners of the church. They attend the meeting places where people gather in that community. They read, listen and observe. They note the languages and learn the traditions of this community. They soak themselves in the cultures of the community that is to be their home for the years ahead. At the end of this period they are ready for the induction service. Invitations are sent to the community leaders visited in the preceding weeks, as well as the usual ecumenical guests. For the first few weeks the pastor's sermons are based on sharing with the congregation the sights and sounds and experiences experienced in community, making the point to the membership that this minister is not for domestication. The Baptist Union must break some of the moulds of ministerial practice that do everything to negate the formation of the missionary pastor. An apostolic church has a commitment to practice the apostolic mission. It is the kiss of death for any community when the church domesticates the ministry and minimises the apostolic calling.[44]

When I read that article, I was stirred in my spirit and said an audible 'Amen'. May others in positions of influence pick up the message and run with it! Pastors have a responsibility for setting the pace of community involvement. There is no alternative to one-to-one involvement in meeting human need. Children may be provided with their own television sets, PlayStations and interactive computers but they need more. They need parents who spend time with them and help them fulfill their potential. Our seniors need more than a comfortable home or residential care. They crave someone who will sit with them, talk to them and listen to them. There is a longing for a sense that they still matter and that they belong. The truth is that no matter what our age or circumstances, we all need human interaction.

Christian disciples need to be encouraged to engage with people systematically and regularly, being the salt and light that the Lord Jesus Christ has called us to be.

The good news is that many local churches are already intimately involved in their community. According to a survey by the Evangelical Alliance:

- 50% of local churches are actively working to care for elderly people and support families.
- 40% are involved in giving comfort and practical help to bereaved members of the community.
- 30% are committed to projects designed to bring about greater community development.
- 10% run either a general advice center or debt counseling center, or provide support for disabled people, housing for some sector of the community or a service offering counseling or education about drug abuse.

Some of the larger churches are involved in all of those areas. That is fine if you have the resources available to do so. Most local churches are not in such a position but nearly all have a building! Small churches are letting their buildings be used as meeting places and function rooms which are in short supply in most communities. That leads us to the second challenge and encouragement before us.

Discover the needs of the community
There is an increasing tendency for local churches to be involved in the wider community. Statutory bodies are often unable to meet legitimate demands or to fulfill their statutory obligation. As such, they are often looking for churches and other charitable organizations to fill the gap.

For instance, Section 72 of the UK Housing Act states that local authorities have to provide suitable housing for needy and vulnerable members of the community, but they are often simply overwhelmed by the need and are unable to fulfill their statutory obligation.

A good starting point for any local church is to go to their local authority and ask what the needs are. Local councilors will certainly be in a position to tell you the things they believe urgently need attention.

Read the local newspapers carefully and regularly over a period of time. Look behind the headlines to the people involved. Gather facts about the problems that are highlighted. Do these stories suggest there are problems caused by the structures of the community?

A simple method of engaging with your community is to conduct a neighborhood survey. It may not reveal all that you need to know but it will be a bridge between the church and the community. A specimen audit form is below for you to consider and adapt to your circumstances.

NEIGHBORHOOD AUDIT

1. What do you like most about living in this area?

2. What are the worst things about this area?
   Is there anything you do not like?

3. Tick how long you have lived in this area:
   under a year [ ]

1–5 years	[ ]
6–10 years	[ ]
11–20 years	[ ]
21–30 years	[ ]
30+ years	[ ]

4. What do you live for? or
   What is the most important thing in life for you?

5. What do you think is the main thing wrong with the world today?

6. How do you think it can be put right?

7. Do churches in this area show much love and care to the people who do not go to church?
   Yes [ ]   No [ ]   Don't know [ ]
   Some [ ]   A little [ ]

8. What needs are there in the community that you think the church should address?

9.
	Yes	No
Is God important to you?	[ ]	[]
If 'Yes', do you go to church?	[ ]	[]

   Which church?

It may well be that you need to set up a small group of activists to carry out this research. Invite observations from church members working in the community. One church adopted this method and came up with the following list. It was useful for social action planning as well as providing material for Sunday worship intercession:

- Lack of awareness of moral standards among young children.
- Increasing number of family problems. Most schools now have family support units. What are we doing to aid this?
- No church in our area has created an employment scheme.
- A need for a social affairs group which will provide information leading to action and protest. This should be done in co-operation with other churches.
- Accommodation problems for students and young people. Many youngsters are exposed to moral danger because of the lack of 'safe' housing.
- The need to support with prayer and encouragement church members in positions of authority and influence in the local community.
- Elderly people living alone. The GP is often the only visitor.

It is of course useless to carry out research unless you have a strategy in place to cope with the findings that come to light. Furthermore, discovering a need does not constitute a call to meet it. The size of the task is so enormous that no single local church can hope to address all needs. That is why all of our ministry and mission must be undergirded by prayer. A church that is in touch with its wider community but out of touch with God is wasting its time. Love God and love other people. Through intercession we discover the area of need that God is calling us to address as a local congregation.

Home Access
Tabernacle Church, Penarth moved into a newly refurbished center in 1990. It was designed to facilitate community

involvement and service as part of God's mission to the town.

Researching the community amongst service providers, Christian or otherwise, revealed that the people in greatest need were homeless single young adults. The office manager at that time had 20 years' experience with the National Children's Homes and was a qualified social worker. He led us into the development of this vital work. Through 1991 'TABS Cares', which had been a program for offering practical assistance to members of our worshiping community, was extended to offer help to the wider community.

Advice was offered on social security benefits and how to secure accommodation for the homeless. The work grew slowly and in 1992 just 41 people had come to us for assistance. However, the word soon got round and in the following year the number had escalated to 109. Usually, the presenting problem for these young people was not having a roof over their heads. But this was never the root problem. In that year, 63% of those seeking help were under the age of 24 and their homelessness was clearly due to the breakdown of family life and the fragmentation of relationships. Often young teenagers could not go home because they were not wanted and parents could no longer cope with them.

The good work done and the results achieved were recognized by the South Glamorgan County Council and the Vale of Glamorgan Council. Grants began to be made to help the work progress:

1. Bond Bank. At the end of 1992 we launched our 'Bond Bank' – the first in Wales. This has proved a very useful service, resolving a problem encountered by many homeless people who, having acquired accommodation, are unable to take up tenancy because they cannot find a bond (at that time it was normally £100 and in 2009 is more likely to be £300). The Bond Bank issues a bond or a promissory note to prospective

landlords, in approved cases, and underwrites any loss, should there be damage caused or arrears of rent. The housing department of the unitary authority, the Vale of Glamorgan Council, has come to depend on our services and for the best part of ten years have given us a grant to fund a part-time bond officer. By 1995 the work had been developed to such an extent that we needed to recruit regular volunteers, some of them coming from other churches. Two other aspects of the work are also now in place.

2. An accommodation finding agency. Many landlords in the town and wider area identify with the work, as a proven way of getting tenants who will pay rent on time and who receive personal support. All properties and landlords are checked to confirm suitability and to maintain high standards.

3. Client support and follow-up. Volunteers visit our clients to offer support, friendship and advice. Settling people into accommodation usually involves having to find furniture, fittings and equipment. Grants are available from various sources but God's work done in God's way always meets with God's provision.

When this work was started, it was costing the church in excess of £20,000 a year. It now costs the church a small fraction of that amount. It has truly been a partnership with statutory authorities and the church is grateful for their interest and for the partnership with the National Assembly of Wales which has also made grants over the past few years.

Our motivation for mission has never changed – it is the love of Christ. By serving the harassed, helpless and hopeless, we seek to show the compassion of our Lord. A few disciples have been made through this work, for which we give God praise and thanks. The overwhelming majority of people with whom we work just take what they need, often without a word of thanks, but it was just like that for our Lord and we can expect no better.

But how rewarding it is to see a homeless person housed, the hurting helped, and sometimes the hopeless finding hope in the Lord Jesus Christ! It has certainly been a wonderful feeder stream to the Alpha Course.

The growth of our work amongst the homeless and needy threatened to make our mission unbalanced. It dominated church meetings and leadership meetings, and could well have split the church. It was claiming an ever-increasing proportion of our church budget as well as time. It certainly caused fragmentation.

At the end of 1995 the full-time social worker left our employ and we now have part-time employees and a good supply of volunteers. All the work is overseen by a very committed Homelessness Management Committee. A separate charitable trust was formed named 'Home Access – Tabernacle Baptist Church, Penarth'. Five trustees and the Homelessness Management Committee have taken over responsibility and accountability for the work. One of the benefits is that it has enabled us to enter into partnerships more easily and to receive grant aid.

Partnerships were formed with the council's housing department, social services and the probationary service.

This is an important part of the mission of the church, but only a part. Although what is being done is a very necessary work, the root cause, social injustice, still has to be attacked. The church still campaigns for better social housing and seeks to address the underlying problems.

Faithworks

I believe Rev. Steve Chalke has been raised up for such a time as this. The organization founded by him, Faithworks, is seeking to engage with political leaders to address the fundamental problems of our society.

Before the general election of 2001 the Faithworks campaign

declaration called on the incoming government:

1. To recognize the important contribution that the local churches and Christian charities had made and can make in providing welfare in the local community.
2. To acknowledge the vital role that faith plays in the motivation and effectiveness of welfare programs developed by churches and Christian charities.
3. To encourage and support the work of local initiatives developing welfare in the community, including those run by churches and other faith-based organizations, and through specific legislation, outcome related monitoring and funding without unnecessary bureaucracy or cost.
4. To ensure that funding criteria for government and local authority grants to projects providing welfare in the local community do not discriminate against the faith that is vital to the success of the work of churches and faith-based organizations.

Steve Chalke writes:

Many local councils know the statutory bodies are fearful that Christians' only interest in welfare work is as a pretext for evangelism and recruitment. All we really care about is 'saving souls', they argue, not 'saving bodies'; Christian welfare work is a thin end of the wedge, leading inevitably and deliberately to a narrow-minded proselytism. But the truth is that our interest in welfare work stems not from a desire to recruit, but from a desire to demonstrate God's love in action. Compassion, not conversion, is the motivation for involvement. Acting on our faith, not telling people about it, is what drives us.

It is important to be up front about this. If our welfare projects are nothing more than underhanded attempts to recruit members – a pretext for proselytism rather than a genuine response to human need – then we should steer well clear. For one thing, our projects themselves are likely to backfire: if those we are helping get the impression that we are being less than honest with them about both our motivation and our aim, they will probably run a mile. And not just from us, but from God as well. By contrast, if they begin to understand and trust that we care for them as whole people, not just souls to be 'counted into the Kingdom', then there is a much better chance they will understand and trust that God cares for them as a whole person too.[45]

Chapter 14

Committed to Reaching the Whole World

Some years ago a missionary conference was held at Moody Church in Chicago. In the large foyer of the church an interesting display was exhibited. It resembled a set of traffic lights with red, amber and green lights that came on and off at intervals. The amber light indicated the departure of missionaries for the foreign field. It came on once every 35 hours. The red light indicated the departure of a lost soul for eternity. It came on three times every two seconds. The green light indicated when every North American church was giving two cents to foreign missions. It came on once every 24 hours. The statistics have certainly changed but the proportions are probably much the same, not only in North America but in the whole northern hemisphere. We should be ashamed.

The Unfinished Task

'Go ye into all the world, and preach the gospel to every creature' (Mark 16:15 KJV). Many years ago I heard the late Stephen Olford preach on this theme and the impact remains to me to this day. He said "When these words were first spoken they were addressed to a small group of people, yet Jesus expected his hearers, and every generation since, to reach the whole world with the Good News of his love. He realized this was no easy task but the command was clear: 'Go ye into all the world, and preach the gospel to every creature.' He knew the great perils the disciples of the cross would have to endure but nevertheless the imperative to go is clear.

It is worth repeating what we have said earlier, that a study of the Great Commission as it appears in the various parts of the

New Testament makes it clear the Lord Jesus meant, quite literally, all the world". [46]

We are to reach every country of the world

Acts 1:8 reminds us that we are to go to the ends of the earth. No country is to be left out. No matter how inaccessible, closed or forbidden, we must penetrate it.

We are to reach every culture of the world

'Therefore go and make disciples of all nations' (Matthew 28:19–20).

The word is 'ethnics'. We live in unique days. Never before in history has such emphasis been placed upon the dignity, unity and sovereignty of individual nations. Great stress is attached to the culture of these nations and, because of this, Christianity is often rejected since it is associated with the culture of the northern hemisphere. Something else that makes today unique is the way in which the nations and cultures of the world are so mobile. Never before has the United Kingdom been made up of so many cultures. This in itself presents a challenge but also a wonderful opportunity to reach other cultures without having to cross any geographical boundaries.

We are to reach every creature of the world

'Go ye into all the world, and preach the gospel to every creature' (Mark 16:15 KJV).

God is no respecter of persons. Therefore, whatever a person's race, class or creed they must be reached with the wonderful message of God's love in Christ. When the Lord Jesus spoke these words, the world was not as accessible to the missionaries as it is today. We therefore have no excuse. The world today is a global village through the miracles of multimedia technology, inexpensive air travel and the advances in literacy and available literature. The task has never been easier. We should hang our heads with shame when we consider there are millions of people who have never heard the gospel of our Lord Jesus Christ.

A healthy church encourages all of its members to be missionaries. For too long we have imagined that the missionary task belongs to a certain favored few, but this is heresy. Every Christian is charged to be a witness. There are hundreds of ways of witnessing and our responsibility is to be a witness in word and deed wherever we find ourselves.

The Unnecessary Hesitancy

We must wonder why global mission has such a low profile in many local churches, especially in light of the priority given to it in the New Testament. Perhaps this hesitancy is due to a number of issues which, in the minds of many Christians, undermine their confidence in the missionary mandate that Jesus gave to the church. Some of these issues are explored below.

Other religions

'Is Christianity the only true revelation of God?'

The prevailing view in a multiracial society is that the church should remain silent for fear of disturbing racial harmony. Our increased knowledge of other religions causes some people to wonder about Christianity's claim to be the definitive revelation of God. More than a few missionaries working overseas have recognized that God has been at work in people's hearts and minds a long time before the Christian gospel arrived. These factors make some Christians hesitant to evangelize people of other faiths.

It is to the scriptures alone that we can turn. Jesus said, 'I am the way and the truth and the life. No-one comes to the Father except through me' (John 14:6). The first apostles preached confidently, 'Salvation is found in no-one else, for there is no other name under heaven given to men by which we must be saved' (Acts 4:12). The conversion of Cornelius recorded for us in Acts chapters 10 and 11 is important for at least two reasons. First, it marks the development of Christianity from a Jewish sect to a worldwide faith and secondly, it marks the opening of the mind of the church to embrace non-Jews.

There was a clear progression in the development of Christianity. Jesus made it clear that the Kingdom of God began with Jews but would not end with them. It was he who sought a Samaritan.

At Pentecost, when the Holy Spirit fell and the church of Jesus Christ was born, it was significant that there were visitors in Jerusalem from all over the then known world. Returning to their homes, they took their newfound faith with them, spreading the Good News as they went. However, the conversion of Cornelius marks a real milestone in the development of Christianity. He was the first full-blooded Gentile to be converted. This led to the founding of a church composed entirely of Gentiles at Antioch and from there to the mission to the whole Gentile world.

To study the first four verses of Acts chapter 10 is to discover several interesting facts about Cornelius. He was God-fearing, devout, and a man of prayer. What is more, God heard his prayers and gave him an angelic revelation and divine direction. Now what is the Christian view of such good, religious people? Perhaps your neighbors are really good people, who believe in God and say their prayers. Do they need saving or do we need to sign them up as allies? The Bible is clear: Cornelius needed saving. Look at Acts 11:14. That is the very reason he was sent to Simon Peter, so that the Apostle could show him the way of salvation.

Christianity has a distinctive message. At the heart of Christianity is a personal relationship with God through Christ. Jesus Christ, the eternal Son of God, came from his Father's home to this earth to do for his creatures what they could not do for themselves. He did not come only to show what God is like, though he did this so perfectly that he could say, 'Anyone who has seen me has seen the Father' (John 14:9). He came to open up the way for sinful, selfish people to enter the presence of God. He came to put away the sin and defilement which would otherwise cut us off from God forever. God's appointed way for him to do this was by going to the cross and dying in the sinner's place. The only sinless man the world has ever known was himself made sin, for us, that we might be made fit for heaven. In a nutshell, that is the Good News. Christ died for us and on the third day rose again. This makes Christianity unique. If Christ is not deity our faith is pathetic and our ministry is redundant. If Christianity is not unique, we have no grounds for mission. If Christ is not Lord, we have no hope. If Jesus Christ is not Savior, we are lost. If Christ is not necessary, we are wasting our time.

This is not to say that other religions are totally devoid of truth. Although they cannot bring you to God, there are elements of truth in all religions and philosophies. But in Christianity alone you will find the whole truth which God has revealed about himself.

Another aspect of Christianity that makes it unique is the coming of the Holy Spirit to make God real to us in our experience. The coming of the Holy Spirit brings power to live. The coming of Christ into a person's life by the power of the Holy Spirit brings the power to transform character and temperament – hallelujah!

May God grant to his church in the twenty-first century a renewed confidence in the gospel that will bring an end to any uncertainty about the uniqueness of our faith. It only serves as a hindrance to the mission of his church.

Hell
'A loving God would never condemn anyone to hell.'

Here is another common statement which has been the means of hindering some from being involved in the mission of the church. We happily embrace the doctrine of heaven and life everlasting, but what of those who die unbelieving? What if I die without Christ? Is there really a hell as well as a heaven?

To be honest, I do not like the idea of hell and I am sure that God does not like the idea of hell either. But do you know that Jesus spoke more about hell than he did about heaven? I accept what Jesus says on any subject, no matter how unpalatable it may seem to be on the surface or how unpopular it may be with others. As surely as there is a heaven to be gained, there is a hell to be avoided. There is such a place, after death, for those who reject Christ, and it is to be avoided at all costs, because once you have entered it, there is no escape from it and no joy in it.

No matter how much the wicked may get away with in this life, a day of reckoning is coming. In fact, were it not for the coming judgment, God might seem either unjust or powerless to exercise his justice in this world which is in such a mess. But cruel and evil people who die unrepentant will go to hell and with them will go all who turn their backs on God, however outwardly respectable they may have been.

Jesus Christ experienced our hell for us on the cross of Calvary. But the writer to the Hebrews challenges us to answer the question, 'How shall we escape if we ignore such a great salvation?' (Hebrews 2:3). The way to escape hell and the way to enter heaven are one and the same. Jesus is the only Savior. May God grant a return to the evangelical faith that preaches the whole counsel of God! This gospel is the only hope for the nations.

Humanitarian needs
'We must be more concerned about the humanitarian needs of the world than we are about saving souls.'

There are some Christians who believe that the principal needs of the nations are social, economic and humanitarian rather than spiritual. It is also true, as stated in previous chapters, that we need to address not just the presenting problems but the root causes. Anyone who knows anything about modern missions will know that these problems are addressed in a holistic fashion. This is not an 'either...or' but a 'both...and' situation. To love our neighbor involves social concern but we demonstrate it most clearly when we share the gospel with them. To send bread and not spiritual food is to communicate that man can live by bread alone. Here the biblical balance is so important and the exact nature of God's love for the nations needs accurate definition.

God's concern is for the whole person – not simply for the saving of souls but the saving of life in every aspect, every relationship and every activity. The will of God touches mind, body and spirit. Compare 2 Corinthians 4:16–18, 5:10–11 and 5:14. Nor must we be content to be involved in agricultural, educational and medical aspects of mission. It is significant that Christian missions are at the forefront of dealing with environmental issues, for God's concern is for the whole of creation. Evangelical Christians ought not to be embarrassed but interested and actively involved in these issues. They matter to God and they should matter to us.

BMS World Mission is the oldest of the modern mission agencies, formed in 1792, and is still considered a leading mission organization. Their mission statement states that their aim is:

- To share life in all of its fullness with the world's people by
- Enabling them to know Christ
- Alleviating suffering and injustice
- Improving the quality of life with people as our primary agents of change – motivating, training, sending and resourcing them.[47]

National churches
'Mission agencies are no longer needed because of the emergence of national churches.'

Thank God those foreign missions have been successful, by the grace of God, in making disciples, in planting churches and helping to establish national churches. No one in their right mind wants to bypass the national church. In the twenty-first century, partnerships between national churches and the mission agencies are the order of the day. Instead of cutting back, however, the opportunities are so great and doors so open that this is a time of missionary expansion. As recently as 15 years ago the Baptist Missionary Society was working in nine countries. Today, however, BMS World Mission supports personnel working in 35 countries across four continents. Their personnel are mostly involved in church planting, education, development, health, disaster relief and media. The world is changing and the needs are increasing.

History of colonialism
'The nineteenth-century missionary movement succeeded largely because of British colonial expansionism and as such it was associated with many evils of colonialism.'

This statement does not tell the whole truth. It is true that Britain as a nation had aspirations to conquer the world for trade and influence. It is also true that there are many things that missionaries and mission agencies have regretted and had to repent over. However, it is wrong to identify missions with the evils of colonialism since missionaries were frequently its staunchest critics. The real truth is that the missionary movement of the nineteenth century was inspired principally and primarily by the revivals of the eighteenth and nineteenth centuries. The revivals at the beginning of the twentieth century also inspired missionary activity. The Christians of those times had a firmer grasp of, and greater confidence in, the biblical doctrine of eternal destiny than we do today.

These, then, are some of the unnecessary hindrances to global mission. We need to repent of wrong thinking. Mission is about going. To be a Christian – a disciple – is to be involved in mission, and the call to mission is the call to go. But going is more a matter of mindset than miles. So let us start thinking straight.

The Unlimited Opportunities

The risen Christ says, 'I have placed before you an open door that no-one can shut' (Revelation 3:8). There are more opportunities for global mission today than there have ever been. We all have opportunities to go, to pray, to give and to inspire.

Opportunities to go

Brian Knell, Church Relations Director of Global Connections and head of Global Options, a consultancy service for churches wanting to be more effective in its Global Mission writes:

> Going in mission is a matter of mindset not miles. There are Christians around who are always thinking about people on the other side of the world. They are constantly in touch. They pray for church fellowships whose language they don't understand. They know about the poor living conditions in the shanty towns outside major cities. They sponsor a child and help provide for their education. They write letters to our Foreign Office about justice issues around the world. But all the time they are physically located in the standard, 1930's semi-detached house in the UK.
>
> Mission is about going. To be a Christian is to be involved in mission and the call to mission is the call to 'go'. But going is more a matter of mindset than miles.
>
> Today there is so much more information to help you go. The TV news regularly brings the world into our front room. If you have access to satellite or cable TV then you're likely to be able to receive Euro News and probably a clear BBC World Radio reception as well. The Internet allows you to access information from all over the globe. Going is a matter of

mindset not miles. But maybe it would be more accurate to say, going is a matter of heart and not hectometres, but then that phrase does not trip off the tongue so well, does it?

The question is, where is your heart? What do you care about? The crisis in Darfur, Sudan is in the news as I write. By the time you read this, the media may have forgotten about Sudan, although the conflict that brings so much grief and death there has been going on for nearly 20 years. If you are a Christian go-er, then other individuals, prisoners, pastors, converts, churches and countries around the globe will cause you to cry, rejoice, smile, pray, give and maybe move your location. So then, fellow Christian, where are you going in mission this week?[48]

God will do great things through you, and in you, if you are willing to be part of the challenge and privilege of world mission. There are still opportunities for life-long missionaries but today there are more short-term mission opportunities than ever before, right on the doorstep, including:

- Summer teams for two to four weeks for church teams; small groups go out for ten days to two weeks
- Action teams for gap year students, usually for about ten months
- Medical teams: opportunities for medical specialists to go for a matter of weeks
- Volunteer programs for individuals and couples to go and spend three months to two years

There are placements available for those with and without professional skills or qualifications. Missionary agencies are looking for people who are:
- Committed Christians with a desire to share their faith and words in actions

- Team players willing to work in partnership with others
- Flexible when situations change shape at short notice
- Servant-hearted and willing to get their hands dirty

If you sense that God may be calling you then here are a few suggestions:

- Talk and pray with your pastor or church leader.
- Contact a mission agency and arrange to see a representative who will tell you of current opportunities, how you will be supported, how you will be prepared and trained, even what you might expect to eat overseas.
- Keep on praying for the Lord to lead you through the scriptures, through Christian counsel and by the prompting of his in-dwelling Holy Spirit.

Opportunities to pray

I am committed to maintaining a world missionary vision. I have a map of the world in my study with photographs of our missionaries serving in various parts of the world. The use of personal prayer letters from missionaries in the field and prayer guides available from mission agencies are all an important part of keeping that vision alive.

Prayer is God's chosen means to do his work. It is also God's chosen means for the church, particularly for the local church, to accomplish his mission. We saw that earlier when we considered the Jerusalem church as a church of prayer.

Paul asked almost every church to pray for him that he might be delivered, that he might have an effective ministry, that he might have boldness and wisdom to proclaim the gospel. A few times, you find the great apostles saying he is depending on their help in prayer. It is God's will that we in our local congregations intercede for those whom God has sent out in mission work around the world.

All small groups should be encouraged to have a missionary for whom they pray and to whom they commit themselves. As we pray, we express our dependence upon God. We say it to God and we show to those around us that we are looking to God and not to people. Perhaps most importantly, we communicate to ourselves that we cannot do God's work without his guidance, his provision and his enabling. When God acts, we do not boast or give credit to ourselves or any human agency. We bow down and worship God and praise him for the answers that we received to our prayers.

We need to pray not only in times of crisis but on a regular basis. We need to pray together and seek God for his mercy and interventions. We need to realize that missionaries in the field, as well as our brothers and sisters of other lands, often face enormous crises. Sometimes it is discouragement, sometimes it is a church, sometimes just the overwhelming challenge of taking the gospel to a people where there is no church and perhaps not even a believer and nothing of the scriptures yet translated into the local language.

Let us recognize these needs and pray together for God's purposes to be fulfilled.

Opportunities to give

A healthy church prioritizes its finances so that a large proportion of it is set aside for the work of mission at home and overseas. If we expect disciples to practice proportional giving in support of the local church local congregations need to practice what they preach. No matter what size the church at least 10% should be set aside for the work of mission. This is not enough to meet all the needs and our target should be not just to increase our giving year-on-year but to increase the proportion of our giving annually.

Sending cannot be accomplished without giving. We teach and encourage the faithful to read and study the Bible, to pray and to witness, but many churches fail to teach stewardship with the same enthusiasm. Jesus Christ is Lord and therefore nothing we possess is ours but his. We are responsible and accountable to God for all that we have and are.

The Apostle Paul writes about the Macedonians who gave spontaneously and pleaded for the privilege of sharing what they had. They promised a gift and made arrangements for its delivery. There is a sense in which what matters is not how much we give but how little we have left.

The Apostle Paul wrote to the Corinthians to remind them of their promise to support the mission of the church. They had failed to deliver and so his letter goes as a reminder to be as quick to give as they were to promise. Do we pay what we promise? We would not go to the bank and tell the manager that we felt our money could be used in better ways than paying off our loan. Yet that is often done with commitments made to missionary giving when we decide that we cannot afford to fulfill our promise. The bank manager has recourse to our capital, but the missionary is stranded with an empty pocket. Of course as circumstances change we are not wrong to ask to be released from our pledge but this should be a last resort. In the same way, missionaries and mission agencies have to demonstrate their good stewardship of what is given.

Stewardship is about lifestyle. We need to ensure that we cannot be accused of robbing God (Malachi 3:8) or deserting those who are depending on us for support.

All of us are called to go; some are called to go overseas and some are called to stay and be witnesses here. All are called to pray. All are called to give. When a call to commitment is made we should all respond, 'Here am I.'

The healthy church has holistic mission as its reason for being. If it doesn't it is only a sick and confused church without a real purpose to exist.

The question must be asked: How can mission be integrated

into every part of church life and not be left as an optional extra to a few committed 'fanatics' on the fringe? Holistic mission must be an integral part of the whole of church life, involving the children, small groups, the leadership and featuring regularly on the agenda of the church meeting.

The leadership of the local church has the primary responsibility for guiding and directing the equipping of the saints for the work of ministry. In closing this chapter, let me suggest a number of ways that will help us to make progress.

Opportunities to inspire

God is a missionary God. Mission is a part of his very being and nature. As God the Father he chose the nation of Israel to be a channel to reach out to a world in rebellion (1 Kings 8:60). He sent his Son to be the Savior of the world. Christ's nature is demonstrated in his birth, life, death and resurrection and his present work of intercession for us. The Holy Spirit's presence at the Day of Pentecost filled those early disciples with the spirit of mission. The whole spectrum of the work of the Trinity from the plan of redemption, made before the world began, to the consummation of all things at the return of Christ, shows us that God has mission as part of his being, character and nature.

The same God is amongst us to inspire us in the twenty-first century. The Holy Spirit inspires us in our worship of a missionary God. The truth about our missionary God needs to be expressed explicitly in our worship, through song, prayers and preaching. As we understand and worship a missionary God, something of the very heart of God becomes our own experience.

The Holy Spirit inspires us through the Bible. God's nature has been expressed historically in action. In the Old Testament we see it expressed in the promises to Abraham, in the Psalms and in the prophets. The whole of the New Testament is the continuation of the missionary plan of redemption. Mission was not the afterthought of the church but part of the pre-determinate counsel of God for the ages. The Bible is the textbook for mission. We need to expose ourselves to it through personal devotional readings but also through the public reading of scripture.

The Holy Spirit inspires God's people through the testimony of his servants. It is important to invite missionaries to come and share what God has done in them and through them. I have had the joy of seeing many offer their lives in Christian service. Invariably God's call has come through God's Word read and preached, and through the testimony of some other faithful servant.

In conclusion, a healthy church is one that recognizes that the missionary call is an unfinished task, overcomes the unnecessary hindrances, and responds to the unlimited opportunities of the ever open door.

'Can these bones live?' God knows they can and he is looking for those who will hear and heed the call to go, to pray, to give and to inspire others in the sharing of the task.

Notes

1   Christian Schwarz, *Natural Church Development*, British Church Growth Association (1996) pp38-9

2   David Beer, *Releasing Your Church To Grow*, Kingsway Publications (2004) p43

3   Rick Warren, *The Purpose Driven Church*, Zondervan (1995) pp340-362

4   Christian Schwarz, *Natural Church Development*, British Church Growth Association (1996) p68

5   Charles Price, *Shaping Tomorrow Starting Today*, Christian Focus Publications (1992) p24

6   Selwyn Hughes, *Discovering Your Place In The Body Of Christ*, Marshalls (1982) p16

7   ibid. p19-20

8   From 'Discovering the Gifts of Church Members', Baptist Union of Great Britain (1996)

9   John Maxwell, *The Power of Leadership*, Eagle Publishing (2002) pp50-51

10 John Maxwell, *The 21 Indispensable Qualities of a Leader*, Thomas Nelson Publishers (1999) pp135-8

11 John Stott, *The Message Of Acts*, Inter-Varsity Press (1990) pp122-3

12 Derek J. Tidball, *Who Are the Evangelicals?* Marshall Pickering (1994)

13 Egyptian Dreams Website on http://www.egyptiandreams.co.uk

14 Larry Crabb in the foreword of Randy Frazee's *The Connecting Church*, Zondervan (2001) pi

15 John Stott, *The Message of Acts*, Acts 2:44–45, Inter-Varsity Press (1990) pp82-3

16 Joseph R. Myers, *The Search to Belong*, Zondervan (2003)

17 Selwyn Hughes, *Every Day with Jesus*, CWR (26 June 1982)

18 ibid. (27 June 1982)

19 ibid. (28 June 1982)

20 David Beer, *Releasing Your Church to Grow*, Kingsway Publications (2004) pp113-3

21 David Beer, *Releasing Your Church to Grow*, Kingsway Publications (2004) pp118-9

22 Christian Schwarz, *Natural Church Development*, British Church Growth Association (1996), pp. 32–33

23 David Beer, *Releasing Your Church To Grow*, Kingsway Publications (2004) p115

24 William Beckham, *The Second Reformation: Reshaping the Church for the 21st Century*, Touch Publications (1997) pp25-6

25 Hymn *"I hear the sound of rustling in the leaves of the tree"* composed by Ronnie Wilson, 1979, Kingsway Thankyou music.

26 William Temple, *The Hope of a New World*, p. 30. Cited by Donald P. Hustad, *Jubilate! Church Music in the Evangelical Tradition* (Carol Stream, Ill.: Hope Publishing Company, 1981), p78.

27 Dr Raymond Brown, *The Message of Nehemiah: The Bible Speaks Today*, Inter-Varsity Press (1998) pp132-3

28 Lyrics by Matt Redman, *The Heart of Worship Files"* Survivor Books, Kingsway Publications (2003)

29 James Montgomery (1771–1854)

30 *The MacArthur New Testament Commentary: Ephesians*, Moody Press (1986)

31 Michael Green, *Mission and Ministry: Obeying Christ in a Changing World*, Fountain Books (1977)

32 *New International Dictionary of New Testament Theology*, Zondervan (1986)

33 *The MacArthur New Testament Commentary: Ephesians*, Moody Press (1986)

34 *Illustrated Bible Dictionary*, Inter-Varsity Press & Tyndale House Publishers (1980)

35 Paul Beasley-Murray, *Radical Leaders*, Baptist Union of Great

Britain (1991) p7

36 This is an ecumenical working group accountable to the Council of Penarth and District CYTUN. The member serving on this group is, however, accountable to the church meeting as are other groups.

37 Film *Forrest Gump*, (1994) Directed by Robert Zemeckis based on the book of the same name by Winston Groom (1986)

38 *"Share the Good News" Workbook*, Bible Society Church Training, England (1988) pp20-23

39 David Beer, *50 Ways to Help Your Church Grow*, Kingsway Publications (2000)

40 Laurence Singlehurst (ed.), *The Evangelism Toolkit*, CWR (1991)

41 *The Vision for Outreach* Volume 7 Institute of Biblical Preaching, Stephen Olford Center, Memphis, USA (1990)

42 Quoted in the sermon *The Vision for Outreach* Volume 7 Institute of Biblical Preaching, Stephen Olford Center, Memphis, USA (1990)

43 Malcolm Muggeridge, *A Third Testament: A modern pilgrim explores the spiritual wanderings of Augustine, Blake, Pascal, Tolstoy, Bonheoffer, Kierkegaard, and Dostoevsky*. Reprinted from www.bruderhof.com. Copyright © 2004 by The Bruderhof Foundation, Inc. Used with permission.

44 *Mainstream* magazine (Summer 2004)

45 Steve Chalke, *Faithworks*, Kingsway Publishing (2001) pp86-7

46 Quoted in the sermon *The Whole Word for the Whole World* Volume 5 Institute of Biblical Preaching, Stephen Olford Center, Memphis, USA (1990)

47 BMS World Mission website is http://www.bmsworld-mission.org

48 As printed in *World Mission*, the magazine of BMS World Mission (November/December 2004)

Bibliography

Beckham, W. A., *The Second Reformation: Reshaping the Church for the 21st Century*, Touch Publications (1997)

Beer, D., *50 Ways to Help Your Church Grow*, Kingsway Publications,

Beer D., *Releasing Your Church to Grow*, Kingsway Publications (2004)

Brierley, P., *The Tide is Running Out*, Christian Research (2000)

Brierley, P., *Pulling Out of the Nose Dive*, Christian Research (2006)

Brown, R., *The Message of Nehemiah: The Bible Speaks Today*, Inter-Varsity Press (1998)

Chalke, S., *Faithworks*, Kingsway Publishing (2001)

Frazee, R., *The Connecting Church*, Zondervan (2001)

Gibbs, E. and Coffey, I., *Church Next*

Gilson, G., *Dead Men Don't Eat Lunch*, fourth edition (2007)

Green, M., *Mission and Ministry: Obeying Christ in a Changing World*, Fountain Books (1977)

Hughes, S., *Discovering Your Place in the Body Of Christ*, Marshalls (1982)

Hughes, S., *Every Day with Jesus*, Crusade for World Revival (1982)

Latourette, K. S., *A History of the Expansion of Christianity*, Eyre & Spottiswoode (1937–1945)

MacArthur, J., *The New Testament Commentary: Ephesians*, Moody Press (1986)

Maxwell, J. C., *The 21 Indispensable Qualities of a Leader*, Thomas Nelson Publishers (1999)

Maxwell, J. C., *The Power of Leadership*, Eagle Publishing (2002)

Muggeridge, M., *A Third Testament*, The Bruderhof Foundation (2004)

Myers, J. R., *The Search to Belong*, Zondervan (2003)

Olford, S.F. *Institute of Biblical Preaching*, Stephen Olford Center,

Memphis, USA (1990) Volumes 5 and 7

Peterson, E. J., *The Message: The Bible in Contemporary Language*, Nave Press (2002)

Price, C., *Shaping Tomorrow Starting Today*, Christian Focus Publications (1992)

Singlehurst, L. (ed.), *The Evangelism Toolkit*, CWR (1991)

Southerland, D., *Transitioning: Leading A Church Through Change*

Stott, J., *The Message of Acts: The Bible Speaks Today*, Inter-Varsity Press (1990)

Tidball, D., *Who Are the Evangelicals?* J. Marshall Pickering (1994)

Wagner, C. P., *Your Spiritual Gifts Can Help Your Church Grow*,

Warren, R., *The Life Development Process*,

Warren, R., *The Purpose Driven Church*, Zondervan (1995)